THEORY OF POLITICAL SOCIOLOGY

About the Author

Prof. S.P. Guru is, at present, emeritus Professor of Political Science at Sambalpur University in the State of Odisha. Born in October 1951, he passed his M.A. in Political Science from Delhi University in 1973 with first-class, and was awarded Ph.D. degree from Sambalpur University in 1990. Professor Guru was a first-class student in all examinations from Matriculation to M.A. and, as such, he is credited with a brilliant academic record throughout his student career. He commenced his professional career as a teacher in Political Science in Sambalpur University, Odisha in 1977, and on rendering 35 years of service as a Post-Graduate University Teacher, and Professor of Political Science, he retired in October 2011 on superannuation. He is a teacher and researcher of national reputation in Political Science.

THEORY
OF
POLITICAL SOCIOLOGY

S.P. Guru
Emeritus Professor of Political Science
Sambalpur University (Odisha)

CONCEPT PUBLISHING COMPANY PVT. LTD.
NEW DELHI-110059

ISBN-13 : 978-93-5125-073-9 (HB)
ISBN-13 : 978-93-5125-074-6 (PB)

First Published 2015

Published and Printed by

Concept Since 1974

Concept Publishing Company Pvt. Ltd.
A/15-16, Commercial Block, Mohan Garden
New Delhi-110059 (India)
T: 25351460, 25351794, *F*: 091-11-25357109
E: publishing@conceptpub.com, W: www.conceptpub.com
Editorial Office: H-13, Bali Nagar, New Delhi-110 015, India.

Cataloging in Publication Data—*Courtesy:* D.K. Agencies (P) Ltd. <docinfo@dkagencies.com>

Guru, Shyama Prasad.
Theory of political sociology / S.P. Guru.
p. cm.
Includes bibliographical references and index.
ISBN 9789351250739 (HB)
ISBN 9789351250746 (PB)

1. Political sociology. I. Title.

DDC 306.2 23

Preface

Aristotle, the Father of Political Science, emphatically opines: "Man is a social animal destined by nature for political life." This statement issued by Aristotle in the 5th Century B.C. amply focuses on the intimate interrelationship between social life and political life; and hence between Society and Politics. As and when Society comes into existence, there emerges the dire necessity of making decisions on societal goals and implementing them effectively. No Society can thrive or continue to exist unless its goals are decided, and also the means of attaining these goals are devised and effectively implemented. As, in reality, there is never obtained complete unanimity of opinions of the people of the Society on its ends and means, there must prevail a decision-making apparatus with its associated process through which decisions on these ends and means would be made, and effectively implemented. Consequently, the situation of conflict emerging from differences of opinions of the people on societal ends and means may be controlled and regulated; and the Society would be enabled to thrive in a situation of peace, order, and stability. Hence, without Society, Politics does not emerge, and also, without Politics, Society cannot thrive and survive. It is this intimate interrelationship between Society and Politics that constitutes the central theme of the newly emerging academic branch of knowledge known as "Political Sociology". It is essentially concerned with a scientific study of "Society-Politics Interactions", and hence, it forms the scientific foundation of the discipline of Political Science.

This book entitled *Theory of Political Sociology* focuses on, and incorporates some major conceptual formulations and frameworks that may be usefully employed by students of Politics in undertaking the study and analysis of "Society-Politics Interactions" by way of discerning the impact of Society on Politics and also the impact of Politics on Society in real-world situations. It comprises ten chapters. Chapter 1 highlights and describes the 'Nature and Scope of Political

Sociology'. Chapter 2 presents a 'Liberal-Democratic Framework' for undertaking realistic study of 'Society-Politics Interactions'. Chapter 3 discusses on the phenomena of 'Influence, Power, and Authority', and Chapter 4 elucidates the 'Political Power-Structure', and these two chapters together constitute the corner-stone of the political process. Chapter 5 delineates the patterns of 'Political-Culture' that tends to determine both micro-politics and macro-politics. Chapter 6 explains the process of 'Political-Socialization' through which people tend to learn patterns of political-culture. Chapter 7 analyzes the process of 'Political-Communication' that disseminates political-information and influences the dynamics of the Political System. Chapter 8 describes the phenomenon of 'Political-Participation' with its determinants that tend to cause it. Chapter 9 focuses on 'Political Movement' that is caused by unconventional and alienated political participation of the people, and discusses its implications for the Political System. Chapter 10 entitled 'Political-Modernization' analyzes the process of modernization of Politics and the emergence of 'Modern Political System' adorned with attributes of political development. These ten chapters are interrelated; and this book containing these ten chapters is characterized by its compactness. It is hoped that it would serve the academic needs of the students of Political Science for a text-book at the B.A.(Hons), M.A., M.Phil., and Ph.D. levels for their core/optional course whether it is entitled 'Political Sociology' or 'Modern Political Theory' or 'Modern Political Analysis'.

In preparing this book, I have been immensely inspired by my respected elder brothers—Prof. Sukadev Nanda and Prof. Brundaban Patel, my most affectionate students-cum-colleagues—Dr. Johani Xaxa, and Dr. Bibhuti Kalyan Mahakul, my wife—Smt. Sita, my sons—Debasis and Subhasis, and my daughters-in-law—Sushree and Shriya. I am thankful to them all. I dedicate this book to my dearest grand-daughter—Akanksha whom I affectionately call as 'NANI'.

I would come to feel that my intellectual endeavour in producing this book is rewarded if the students and teachers of the discipline of Political Science would be benefited by it in their academic pursuits.

February 4, 2014 (Basant Panchami) **Prof. S.P. Guru**

Sri Niketan,
Sri Ram Vihar, Burla-768020.

Contents

1

Political Sociology: Nature and Scope of Study

Political Sociology is an academic branch of knowledge concerned with the study and analysis of the interactions between Society and Politics. As such, it involves an academic-endeavour for understanding the dynamics of the Political Society as well as the role of the individual in it on enquiring into, and discerning reciprocal influences between Society and Politics. Its emergence, as a formal academic concern, may be traced, as scholars such as W.G. Runciman[1] and SM. Lipset[2] point out, to the middle of the Nineteenth Century. However, its intellectual antecedents may be found dating as far back as to the 5th Century B.C.

1.1 Intellectual Antecedents

From the time of recorded history, especially from 5th Century B.C. onwards, intellectuals and scholars are concerned with the study of the State on enquiring into, and discerning the impact of societal structure and culture upon it. For instance, Plato[3] (427 B.C.-347 B.C.) in his book '*Republic*' identifies three classes of people of the Society such as the Producing Class, the Military Class, and the Ruling Class that determine the nature, structure and functions of his Ideal State. His concept of the Ideal Political Society is based on the fundamental premise of integration between Society and State. This fundamental premise is followed by his pupil Aristotle[4] (384 B.C.-322 B.C.) who in his book '*The Politics*' analyses the reciprocal relationship between

Society and State by way of identifying the socio-economic factors such as family, class, status, education, and occupation as vital determinants of political stability or change. He also simultaneously focuses on the nature of public policies and the temper of the government as crucial variables of social cohesion and integration.

The integrated approach in envisioning and analyzing Society-State relationship, as pioneered by the Ancient Greek Scholars during the classical period, was questioned during the Middle-Ages (Medieval Period), especially during the period of the Enlightenment that commenced with the renaissance in the Twelfth Century and followed thereafter till the end of the Fifteenth Century. During this period, the dichotomy between Society and State was focused, and the supremacy of the State *vis-à-vis* the Society was asserted. This trend was subsequently followed by scholars, and reflected in their intellectual endeavours. For instance, Niccolo Machiavelli[5] (1469 A.D.-1527 A.D.) in his book '*The Prince*' emphasizes on the autonomy and sovereignty of the Ruler of the State in manipulating social institutions such as 'Religion' and 'Nobility' for the purpose of establishing and maintaining political stability as well as his own strength and greatness. Also, Thomas Hobbes[6] (1588 A.D.-1679 A.D.) in his book '*Leviathan*' asserts the exclusive supremacy and absoluteness of the Ruler in his relationship with the people, and in conditioning the Society as well. However, John Locke[7] (1632 A.D-1704 A.D.) in his book '*Second Treatise on Civil Government*' highlights on the existence of Society prior to the State, and focuses on the supremacy of the Society *vis-à-vis* the State on proclaiming the doctrine of popular sovereignty. Also, Jean Jaques Rousseau[8] in his book '*The Social Contract*' emphasizes on societal control over State and Government through his concept of 'General Will'.

The philosophical assertion of societal influence on State and Politics was empirically reinforced, for the first time, in the mid of the Nineteenth Century, in the works of two great intellectuals such as Karl Marx (1818 A.D.-1863 A.D.) and Max Weber (1864-1920). Marx[9], in his monumental works such as '*Das Capital*' and '*Communist Manifesto*', focuses on the economic factor as the exclusive determinant of the nature and structure of the State, and of the process of politics in the society as well; but Weber[10] discerns social factors such as status, culture (belief system), and social groups as the vital determinants of the structure of State-Authority and the nature of public policy. The empirical identification of socio-economic factors, and assertion of their determining roles in conditioning politics brought about a total transformation in intellectual pursuits from normative and philosophical perspectives to realistic and scientific perspectives in analyzing and understanding Society-Politics relationship. Because of these pioneering contributions of Karl Marx and Max Weber, the foundation of Scientific Political Sociology was laid down, and hence, they may be acknowledged as its founding fathers.

The new trend for scientific study of Society-Politics relationship as initiated by Marx and Max Weber was reinforced, developed, and followed up subsequently by a large number of scholars and intellectuals. In this context, Sociologists as well as Political Scientists have immensely contributed for the further growth and development of 'Scientific Political Sociology'. For instance, during the later part of the Nineteenth Century and the first part of the Twentieth Century, contributions of scholars and intellectuals such as Vilfredo Pareto (1848-1923), Gaetano Mosca (1858-1941), Robert Michels (1876-1936), Emile Durkheim (1858-1917), Karl Mannheim (1893-1947), Grahamwallas, Arthur F. Bentley and Charles E. Merriam are of great significance. Pareto's[11] work '*The Mind and Society*', Mosca's[12] work '*The Ruling Class*', Michels'[13] work '*Political Parties*', Durkheim's[14] work '*Professional Ethics and Civil Morals*', Mannheim's[15] work '*Man and Society in an Age of Reconstruction*', Grahamwalla's[16] work '*Human Nature in Politics*', Bentley's[17] work '*The Process of Government', and Merriam's*[18] work '*New Aspects of Politics*' address to, and direct for a realistic study of Politics on enquiring into its sociological and psychological bases.

Because of the impact of these scientific orientations, there emerged, in the discipline of Political Science, an intellectual movement known as 'Behavioural Movement'[19] in the period that followed the end of Second World War in 1945. The consequences of the Second World War necessitated socio-economic and political reconstructions in the war-damaged states, and for this purpose, there were invited plans, schemes, and models from the intellectuals belonging to various academic disciplines. However, for solving and mitigating the then emerging pressing needs of mankind, Political

Scientists could not contribute meaningfully because of inadequacies of conventional approaches and methods of political analysis[20] characterized overwhelmingly by normativism, or formalism including legalism, and institutionalism. Hence, in the quest for social relevance, academic endeavours were undertaken for founding the 'science' of Politics on undertaking a realistic and scientific study of political behaviour at the level of the individual, groups and collectivities, as well as institutions. For this purpose, scholars re-oriented their academic focus on the enquiry and discernment of linkages between political phenomena and their sociological determinants, and also between societal structure and its political determinants. The Behavioural Approach to the study of Politics, fortified by Sociological Theories, indeed, immensely contributed for instituting the discipline of Political Sociology formally in different Universities in the period that followed 1945.[21] For its growth, significant academic contributions, both theoretical and empirical, were rendered by a large number of Political Scientists such as: Harold D. Lasswell,[22] David Easton,[23] Gabriel A. Almond,[24] James S. Coleman,[25] Sidney Verba,[26] G.B. Powell Jr.[27] David Truman[28], Lucian W. Pye[29], Robert A. Dahl[30], Karl W. Deutsch[31] David E Apter,[32] and Sociologists such as Talcott Parsons[33], S.M. Lipset[34], R. Bendix[35], W.G. Runciman[36], W.J. M. Mackenzie[37], Robert K. Merton[38], Robert E. Lane[39], Lewis A. Coser[40], Scott Greer[41], Peter Orleans[42], Richard G. Braungart[43], Anthony M. Orum[44], Tom Bottomore[45], S.N. Eisenstadt[46], Cyril E. Black[47], C. Wright Mills[48], Robert E. Dowse[49], John A. Hughes[50], Morris Janowitz[51], Giovanni Sartori[52], and many others. Thus, since 1945, the discipline of Political Sociology is being increasingly enriched by the contributions, both theoretical and empirical, of Political Scientists as well as Sociologists.

1.2 Nature of Political Sociology

The nature of Political Sociology may be discerned and described keeping in view its genesis and in-born qualities. Political Sociology, as an academic branch of knowledge, seems to have emerged as a consequence of the employment of sociological theories and approaches to the study of political phenomena, and also of the political models and approaches to the study of societal-structure and culture. As Giovanni Sartori rightly points out: "Political Sociology is only born when the sociological and politological approaches are combined at their point of intersection."[53] In view of the genesis of Political Sociology, Sartori aptly defines it as "an interdisciplinary hybrid"[54] born out of "a balanced cross-fertilization"[55] between the disciplines of Sociology and Political Science. It seems to combine social and political explanatory variables in studying politico-sociological phenomenon. It treats societal structure and culture as explanatory variables of political phenomena, and also considers political structures, policies, and process as explanatory variables of societal structures and culture. As such, it is involved with the study of reciprocal influences and inter-penetration between Society and Politics, and tends to integrate the findings for understanding the dynamics of the Political Society.

As Political Sociology is the academic offspring of both Sociology and Political Science, it is quite natural for it to inherit the essential attributes of its parents. Therefore, the nature of Political Sociology may be meaningfully understood and appreciated on discerning, analyzing and synthesizing the essential attributes of both Sociology and Political Science.

1.2.1 Essential Concerns of Sociology

The discipline of Sociology, in general, is concerned with the study of the Society and its dynamics as a whole. Society, as Leon H. Mayhew defines, "is a relatively independent or self-sufficient population characterized by internal organization, territoriality, and cultural disinctiveness"[56] For performing its diverse functions, it creates various systems and institutions which may be classified into three major types such as the Social System, the Economic System and the Political System. However, each of these systems is composed not of individuals but of their distinctive roles, and hence the individual remains as the basic unit of the Society. Of course, the individual tends to perform social, economic, and political roles as and when required, and consequently, the Society is enlivened and it becomes dynamic. As the roles of the individual are not exclusive but interrelated, there ensues a process of reciprocal influences among the Social System, the Economic System, and the Political System of the Society. Thus, the Society as a whole becomes characterized by reciprocal influences and interpenetration among its various systems and institutions. Hence, the study of Society involves, as Talcott Parsons[57] emphasizes, the totality of the societal process including all roles, and behaviour of the members of these institutions, and their inter-relationship.

As such, the essential concern of the discipline of Sociology is the study and analysis of human behaviour and interactions in societal context. However, systematic and scientific study of human behaviour at the level of individual as well as the collectivity inevitably involves an enquiry into human psychology and sociology because behaviour is the outcome of the individual's psychology or mind-set which, in turn, tends to be formed and shaped by his sociological identities and traits such as race, ethnicity, caste, class, language, religion, age, gender, income, occupation, societal culture etc. Thus, in the context of formation and development of the individual's psychology characterized by a distinctive pattern of orientations towards societal objects, what may be termed as culture[58], his sociological traits and identities seem to play crucial and determining roles. Of course, the process of formation of the individual's culture tends to be significantly influenced not only by his sociological attributes but also by the roles of various agents and institutions with whom the individual interacts during his life-span. Hence, the process of socialization involving the roles of varieties of socializers such as family, school and educational institutions, peer group, mass-media, voluntary groups, jobs and occupations, and the totality of the socio-economic and political environment need be enquired into, and the extent of their impact upon the individual in the context of formation of his personality and mind-set need be examined and analyzed for understanding human behaviour meaningfully. Thus, both psychology and sociology of the individual seem to be vital determinants of his behaviour. Hence, the study of human behaviour in societal context, (that being the prime concern of the discipline of Sociology), inevitably involves a systematic, scientific and logical enquiry into the personality traits, the pattern of culture, and the process of socialization of the individual and the collectivity. At the same time, as human behaviour and roles make the various systems and institutions of the society operational and dynamic in the context of societal goal-attainment, the discipline of Sociology is also vitally concerned with the study of the issues of societal stability, development, modernization, and change.

1.2.2 Essential Concerns of Political Science

The discipline of Political Science is vitally concerned with the scientific study of Politics. For a succinct identification of the essential attributes of Politics, we may adopt the notion of David Easton who defines Politics as the process of "authoritative allocation of values for a society".[59] As Easton points out, for every society, and in every society, there operates a process through which values, i.e. preferences of the people expressed in the form of demands on public issues, are sought to be authoritatively allocated. Public issues are the issues that pertain to the people the Society as a whole, and may be classified, for the sake of convenience, into four broad categories such as those that concern societal organization, societal leadership, societal domestic policies, and societal foreign policies.[60] On these public issues, people tend to form preferences, and opinions, (as to what should or should not be done) that may be termed as 'values', and these are expressed as demands for making of authoritative decisions or public policies. However, as regard the desires and demands of the people on societal issues, there is found, in reality, no unanimity but differences of opinions, and hence, there emerges the necessity for authoritative allocation of values. These allocations and decisions on values are made by the Authority or Government of the Society for the people as a whole, and are known as authoritative allocations because these are backed by legitimate sanctions of the former. Only when the allocations become authoritative or legitimately binding, these become capable of effective implementation as disobedience would entail punishment for the disobedient and the deviant. Consequently, effective implementation of authoritative decisions would, most likely, prevent anarchy and chaos in Society, and facilitate the establishment of societal order, stability and viability.

Politics, thus viewed as the process of authoritative allocation of values for a Society, involves performance of three major types of interrelated activities, and roles[61] of the people such as: (i) those that relate to the way values (preferences and demands of the people on societal issues) come to be formulated, and the Authority or Government of the Society is made aware of them, (ii) those that relate to the way the Authority of the Society digests the values and makes authoritative decisions, and (iii) those that relate to the way authoritative decisions are effectively implemented in the Society for attainment of societal goals. Therefore, the most distinguishing attribute of Politics is the performance of one or more of these three major types of activities, behaviour, and roles at the level of the individual or institutions. Politics may be said to have become functional when individuals, collectivities and institutions make demands upon the Government for making of authoritative decisions as desired by them on various societal issues, and when the incumbents of Government make authoritative decisions on these demands and implement them. Thus viewed, Government is the corner-stone of Politics as the entire process of authoritative allocation of values revolves round the pivot of Government; and therefore, Politics is centrally concerned with the inter-play of 'Power-behaviour' at the level of the individual, groups and the Government of the Political system.

Hence, the study of Politics of a Society essentially involves the study of both 'Micro-politics' and 'Macro-politics'.[62] Political activities undertaken by the individual and the groups may be termed as micro-politics; whereas activities relating to authoritative allocation of values undertaken by the Government as the Authority of the Political System of the Society may be termed as macro-politics. Micro-politics and Macro-politics are interrelated because political activities and behaviour of the individuals tend to influence and determine the pattern of performance of the Political System in the context of authoritative allocation of values for the Society. Both Micro-politics and Macro-politics, however, are to be studied scientifically by the discipline of Political Science as, by its very nomenclature, it is essentially concerned with scientific study of Politics. Since scientific study involves observation, investigation, experimentation, comparison and generalization on phenomena, factual data concerning the observed and observable political process at both the micro and macro levels are to be collected on the employment of scientific methods of data collection, and the data, thus collected, are to be analyzed and examined objectively on the application of scientific techniques of data-analysis, and then, generalizations in the form of theories and models may be conceptualized, and be subjected to further testing and refinement.

1.2.3 Essential Concerns of Political Sociology

Political Sociology, being the academic hybrid of both Sociology and Political Science, seeks to synthesize harmoniously the essential concerns of its parental disciplines. The discipline of Sociology is essentially concerned with the study of human behaviour in societal context; whereas the discipline of Political Science is essentially concerned with the study of 'power-behaviour', i.e. human behaviour in the context of authoritative allocation of values for the Society. These essential academic concerns of both Sociology and Political Science are sought to be synthesized by Political Sociology which, as a consequence, tends to be essentially concerned with the study of 'power-behaviour' in 'societal context'. As Tom Bottomore emphatically points out: "......... The principal object of political sociology has been, and should be, the phenomenon of power at the level of an inclusive society".[63] Bottomore notices the inter-play of legitimate power, what may be termed as power-behaviour, in every inclusive society that is characterized by self-sustaining growth and development as well as internal supremacy and external independence in the context of making of authoritative decisions and public policies. According to him, the study of 'Power-behaviour' or 'Politics' in relation to the Society, and the *viceversa*, and also the building of linkages between political and social life are the central academic concerns of Political Sociology.

1.3 Scope of Political Sociology

The scope of Political Sociology may be discerned and delineated in accordance with its genesis, nature, and essential academic concerns. As it is the interdisciplinary progeny of the established disciplines of Political Science and Sociology, and is centrally concerned with building of linkages between social and political life, Political Sociology is involved with the study of interactions between Society and Politics.

In this context, the notions of the following distinguished scholars may be noted.

Giovanni Sartori: "Political Sociology is an interdisciplinary hybrid attempting to combine social and political explanatory variables......"[64]

Morris Janowitz: "Broadly conceived, political sociology is concerned with the social basis of power in all institutional sectors of society" as it deals with "the patterns of social stratifications and their consequences in organized politics", and simultaneously, it also treats "political institutions as....independent sources of societal change".[65]

Richard G. Braungart: "Political Sociology is the attempt to understand and explain political society" and is generally defined as "study of the relationship between Society and Politics". More specifically it enquires into and studies the dynamic associations among and between (1) the Social origins of politics, (2) the structure of politics or the political process, and (3) the effects of politics on the surrounding society and culture".[66]

Michael Rush and Philip Althoff: Political Sociology is concerned with "the examination of the links between politics and society, between social structures and political structures, and between social behaviour and political behaviour".[67]

Robert E. Dowse and John A. Hughes: Political Sociology is "mainly concerned with the analysis of the interaction between politics and society".[68] It involves "the study of political behaviour within a sociological perspective or frame-work"[69], but it is "not an activity of social reductionism which reduces political events to by-products of the social, but sees the problem as one of interaction between the social and the political".[70.] It examines not only "the effect various social factors have on political life" but "it is also clear that political institutions, like government, bureaucracies, parliaments and so on, while they are embedded in a social net-work, in their turn, influence the social system of which they are a part."[71]

Anthony Orum: Political Sociology enquires into "how politics both is shaped by and shapes other events in societies."[72]

Tom Bottomore: Political Sociology is concerned with systematic inquiry into "the relations between political and social life."[73]

An analysis of these above-mentioned notions amply indicates that Political Sociology, as an academic branch of knowledge, is earnestly concerned with the study of interactions between Society and Politics on enquiring into and exploring the influence of Society on Politics as well as the influence of Politics on Society for the purpose of understanding and explaining the dynamics of the Political Society. Accordingly, the scope of Political Sociology involves a two-way process of relationship between Society and Politics.

SOCIETY ⇄ POLITICS

Political Sociology, therefore, considers sociological variables such as societal structure, culture, and social identities of individuals and collectivities as explanatory variables and determinants of political phenomena, and it also treats political-structure, policies, and process as determinants of societal culture, societal organization, and its change and development. It seeks to enquire into how Society influences Politics, and also how Politics influences Society. Basing on these findings as to the interactions between Society and Politics, it seeks to build hypotheses, theories, and models in the quest for a comprehensive understanding of the dynamics of the Political Society.

This comprehensive scope of Political Sociology amply distinguishes it from Sociology of Politics. In this context, there may be noted, as mentioned below, the notions of some scholars such as Reinhard Bendix and S.M. Lipset, Lewis Coser, Samuel Greer and Peter Orleans who narrow down the scope of Political Sociology, and misconstrue it with the scope of Sociology of Politics.

Reinhard Bendix and S.M. Lipset: "…. Political Sociology starts with society and examines how it affects the state."[74]

Lewis Coser: "Political Sociology is that branch of Sociology which is concerned with the social causes and consequences of given power distribution within or between societies, and with the social and political conflicts that lead to changes in the allocation of power."[75]

Samuel Greer and Peter Orleans: "Political Sociology would seem to be simply the sociological study of politics"[76] and it is mostly concerned with description, analysis and sociological explanation of the peculiar social structure called the State."[77]

These notions essentially focus on a description of the scope of Sociology of Politics, not of the scope of Political Sociology. Sociology of Politics is exclusively concerned with the study of one-way process of relationship between Society and Politics; it considers sociological variables as the explanatory variables of political phenomena which are treated as dependent on and determined by the former. It is unconcerned with the study of the impact of Politics upon Society. Thus, as Giovani Sartori rightly points out, Sociology of Politics is 'a sociological reduction of politics',[78] and hence, its scope of study is narrow and limited.

As distinguished from Sociology of Politics, Political Sociology is much wider and comprehensive in its scope of study, and hence, it cannot be considered as a synonym for Sociology of Politics.[79] As an academic discipline, its scope involves the study and analysis of interactions, interrelations, and reciprocal influences between Society and Politics. It undertakes the study of Politics on enquiring into their sociological bases, and simultaneously, it enquires into the impact of Politics upon the Society as a whole. While undertaking the study of Politics, both at the micro and macro levels, sociological bases and determinants are necessarily enquired into, discerned, and the extent of their impact upon micro-politics and macro-politics is examined and measured. At the level of macro-politics, the dynamics of the Political System is sought to be analyzed on enquiring into the functions of interest-articulation, interest-aggregation, rule-making, rule-application, rule-adjudication, political communication, and political socialization as performed by their corresponding structures such as pressure-groups, political parties, legislature, executive, judiciary, mass-media, and political-socializers. It also involves an enquiry into the level of political modernization, political development, or change of the Political System. On the whole, the over-all performance of the Political System is sought to be analyzed on enquiring into, and examining the impact of societal structure and culture upon it. Thus, Political Sociology is essentially involved with the study and analysis of Politics at both micro and macro levels, on enquiring into, and examining the impact of Society upon them. It considers societal culture and structure as determinants and explanatory variables of political phenomena, and undertakes a study of their interrelationships. At the same time, Political Sociology is also involved with a study and analysis of the impact of Politics upon societal-structure and culture, and also the role of the Political System in the process of societal modernization, development, and change. As S.M. Lipset, on reconsideration, emphatically opines: "Political Sociology is not solely the study of social factors that condition the political order. Indeed political institutions are themselves social structures, and hence are often independent (that is causal) factors that affect non-political social structure"[80]. In this context, also Richard G. Braungart upholds: ".... Society is made up of a web of social institutions whose structures and functions overlap and interact with one another. Politics and power are the dynamic components of these relationships, which articulate the interdependence and competition between social needs and goals in the value system, the institutional or organizational means to achieve these goals, and the pattern of interactions that result."[81] This point of view that Political Sociology is concerned with the study not only of the impact of Society on Politics but also of the impact of Politics upon Society is focused and asserted by other scholars among whom Giovanni Sartori[82] seems to be the pioneer.

On the whole, Political Sociology is essentially concerned with the enquiry, examination and analysis of reciprocal influences between Society and Politics on considering each as the explanatory variable for the other. For instance, in undertaking the study of a political phenomenon such as voting behaviour of the people of a Democratic Political System, the Political Sociologist enquires into the intensity of their allegiance to the primary and secondary social groups formed on the basis of social identities such as race, ethnicity, caste, tribe, religion, language, and class etc., and examines the impact of these sociological factors upon the voters in conditioning their voting behaviour. Simultaneously, it is also the concern of the Political Sociologist to enquire into, and to examine the impact of the prevalent democratic principles and values such as universal adult franchise, political rights and liberty, and the openness of the Political System etc. upon societal structure and culture in facilitating and furthering the democratization of social groups and their political mobilization, and also in founding and strengthening the Civil Society. Similarly, the study of the phenomenon of communal politics involves not only an examination of the impact of religious beliefs and behaviour of the individual and groups upon both micro-politics and macro-politics but also an examination of the impact of Politics upon religious groups in the context of their political mobilization.

Thus, Political Sociology seeks to build linkages and bridges between Society and Politics on enquiring into, and assessing scientifically the impact of Society upon Politics as well as the impact of Politics upon Society. This academic endeavour, therefore, involves a scientific study of "Society-Politics Interactions". For this purpose, relevant realistic data or facts are collected on employing scientific methods of data-collection such as the Survey Research Method, Sample Survey, Case Study, Interview, Questionnaire, and Participant-observation etc. The data, thus collected, are then subjected to quantitative measurement and analysis on employing scientific techniques of data-measurement such as calculator, precision-scale, and the computer etc. The findings are subsequently subjected to objective analysis, free from value-biases and prejudices, and tested again and again in order to ascertain their universal validity and relevance, and basing on these findings, theories and models are constructed. These theories and models are employed for analyzing and understanding Society-Politics Interactions, and are refined or changed in accordance with new empirical findings.

Hence, Political Sociology, as the academic offspring of the disciplines of Sociology and Political Science, is essentially concerned with search for realism, search for precision, search for comprehensiveness, search for universalism, and search for intellectual orders because it is ardently devoted to a realistic, scientific, and comprehensive study of the interactions between Society and Politics; and basing on these investigations and analyses, it seeks to construct models and theories for meaningfully understanding the socio-political process, and the dynamics of the Political Society. As Political Sociology is essentially involved with scientific enquiry and analysis of Politics, its scope of study seems to be identical with that of Science of Politics or Political Science; and these two nomenclatures, "Political Sociology" and "Political Science", as Maurice Duverger[83] emphatically points outs, are almost synonymous. Hence, today, Political Scientists, as H.V. Wiseman[84] rightly observes, tend to look to Political Sociology as a renewed centre of the discipline of Political Science.

REFERENCES

1. W.G. Runciman, *Social Sciences and Political Theory*. (London: Cambridge University Press, 1963), Chapter-2.
2. S.M. Lipset: *Political Man*. (London: William Heinemann Ltd., 1960), Chapter-I, p. 22.
   ——Also, 'Political Sociology' in R.K. Merton, L. Broom and L.S. Cortell (eds), *Sociology Today: Problems and Prospects*. (New York: Harper Torch Books, 1953), p. 181.
3. Plato, *Republic*, Translated by Benjamin Jowett (Oxford: Oxford University Press, 1953).
4. Aristotle, *The Politics*; Translated by Benjamin Jowett (Oxford: Clarendon Press, 1905).
5. Niccolo Machiavelli, *The Prince*, Translated by N.H. Thompson. (Oxford: Clarendon Press, 1913).
6. Thomas Hobbes, *Leviathan*. With an Introduction by Michael J. Oakeshott. (Oxford: Blackwell, 1946).
7. John Locke, *The Second Treatise on Civil Government*. With an Introduction by John W. Gough (Oxford: Blackwell, 1946).
8. Jean Jaques Rousseau, *The Social Contract*. Translated by John W. Gough. (Oxford: Clarendon Press; 1936).
9. Karl Marx, *Das Capital*. Reprinted (Moscow: Foreign Language Publishing House, 1961).
   ——, *Communist Manifesto*. Reprinted. (Moscow: Progress Publisher, 1975).
10. Max Weber: *The Theory of Social and Economic Organization*. Translated by A.M. Handerson and Talcott. Parsons. (Glencoe: Free Press, 1947).
11. Vilfredo Pareto, *The Mind and Society* (New York: Harcourt-Brace, 1935).
12. Gaetano Mosca, *The Ruling Class*, (ed.) A. Livingston. (New York: McGraw-Hill, 1939).
13. Robert Michels, *Political Parties: A Sociological Study of the Oligarchical Tendencies of Modern Democracy* (Glencoe, Illinois: The Free Press, 1942). Translated in English in 1915.
14. Emile Durkheim, *Professional Ethics and Civil Morals*. Translated by C. Brookfield (Glencoe, Illinois: Free Press, 1960).
15. Karl Mannheim, *Man and Society in an Age of Reconstruction*. Translated by E. Shills. (New York: Harcourt, Brace and World, 1940).
16. Graham Wallas, *Human Nature in Politics* (London: Constable Press, 1908).
17. Arthur F. Bentley, *The Process of Government* (Chicago: Chicago University Press, 1908).

18. Charles E. Merriam, *New Aspects of Politics* (Chicago: Chicago University Press, 1925).
19. David Easton, A Framework for Political Analysis (Englewood Cliff, N.J.: Prentice-Hall, 1965), p. 4.
    See, Also, Robert A. Dahl, "The Behavioural Approach in Political Science: Epitaph for a Monument to a Successful Protest", *The American Political Science Review*, No. 55, 1961, pp. 763-772, esp, p. 765.
20. Robert A. Dahl, "The Behavioural Approach in Political Science...." *Op. cit.* p. 764.
21. *Ibid*., p. 764, Also
    (i) W.G. Runciman: *Social Science and Political Theory*. (London: Cambridge University Press, 1963) Chapt. 2.
    (ii) S.M. Lipset, 'Political Sociology' in Robert K. Merton, L. Brown and Leonard S. Cottrel. Jr. (eds.), *Sociology Today*. (New York: Harper, 1965), p. 81.
22. Harold D. Lasswell:
    (i) *Politics: Who Gets What, When, How*. (NewYork: McGraw-Hill, 1936).
    (ii) *The Analysis of Political Behaviour: An Empirical Approach* (London: Kegan Paul, 1947).
    (iii) *Power and Society—A Framework for Political Analysis*. (New Haven: Yale University Press, 1950) in collaboration with Abraham Kaplan.
    (iv) *The Future of Political Science* (New York: Atherton Press, 1963).
23. David Easton:
    (i) *The Political System: An Enquiry into the State of Political Science* (New York: Alfred A. Knopf, 1953).
    (ii) *A Framework for Political Analysis*. (Englewood Cliffs, N.J.: Prentice-Hall, 1965).
    (iii) *A Systems Analysis of Political Life*. (New York: Wiley, 1965).

24-25. Gabriel A. Almond and James, S. Coleman (eds.), *The Politics of the Developing Areas*. (Princeton, N.J.: Princeton University Press, 1960).

26. Gabriel A. Almond and Sidney Verba, *The Civic Culture* (Princeton, N.J.: Princeton University Press, 1963).
27. Gabriel A. Almond and G.B. Powell, Jr. *Comparative Politics: A Developmental Approach* (Boston: Little, Brown & Co, 1966).
28. David B. Truman: (i) 'The Implications of Political Behavioural Research', *Item*, Vol. 5 (1951) pp. 37-39.
    (ii) *The Governmental Process* (New York: Alfred. A. Knopf, 1951).
29. Lucian W. Pye:
    (i) *Communications and Political Development*. (Princeton, N.J.: Princeton University Press, 1963). Edited with Sidney Verba.

(ii) *Political Culture and Political Development.* (Princeton, N.J.: Princeton University Press, 1965).
(iii) *Aspects of Political Development.* (Boston: Little Brown & Co, 1966).

30. Robert A Dahl:
    (i) 'A Critique of the Ruling Elite Model'. *American Political Science Review*, Vol. 52, 1958, pp. 463-469.
    (ii) Who Governs? (New Haven: Yale University Press, 1961).
    (iii) *A Preface to Democratic Theory.* (Chicago: Chicago University Press, 1961).
    (iv) 'The Behavioural Approach in Political Science....' *The American Political Science Review*, No. 55, 1961, p. 763-772.
    (v) *Polyarchy: Participation and Opposition* (New Haven: Yale University Press, 1971).
    (vi) *Modern Political Analysis* (Englewood Cliffs, N.J.: Prentice-Hall, 1963).
31. Karl W. Deutsch, *Nerves of Government: Models of Political Communication and Control* (New York: The Free Press, 1963).
32. David E. Apter, *The Politics of Modernization.* (Chicago: Chicago University Press, 1965).
33. Talcott Parsons:
    (i) *The Structure of Social Action.* (New York: McGraw-Hill, 1937).
    (ii) *The Social System.* (Glencoe, Illinois: The Free Press, 1951).
    (iii) *Politics and Social Structure* (New York: The Free Press, 1969).
34. S.M. Lipset:
    (i) *Political Man: The Social Bases of Politics* (London: William Heinemann, 1960).
    (ii) *Politics and the Social Sciences* (ed). (New York: Oxford University Press, 1969).
35. Reinhard Bendix:
    (i) 'Political Sociology' An Essay and Bibliography in Current Sociology (Paris: UNESCO, 1957) Vol. 6, (in collaboration with S.M. Lipset).
    (ii) *State and Society: A Reader in Comparative Political Sociology.* (Boston: Little, Brown & Co., 1968) Edited.
36. W.G. Runciman: *Social Science and Political Theory.* (London: Cambridge University Press, 1963).
37. W.J.M. Mackenzie, *Politics and Social Science* (London: Penguin, 1967).
38. Robert K. Merton, *Social Theory and Social Structure.* (Glencoe, Illinois: The Free Press, 1949).
39. Robert E. Lane, *Political Life: Why People Get Involved in Politics.* (Glencoe, Illinois: The Free Press, 1959).

40. Lewis A. Coser (ed), *Political Sociology*. (New York: Harper Row, 1966).
41-42. Scott. Greer and Peter Orleans, 'Political Sociology' in R.L. Faris (ed.), *Handbook of Modern Sociology*. (Chicago: Rand Macnally & Co, 1964).
43. Richard. G. Braungart:
    (i) Society and Politics: Readings in Political Sociology. (New Jersey: Princeton-Hall 1975). Edited.
    (ii) 'Political Sociology' in Samuel Long (ed) *Handbook of Political Behaviour*, Vol. 3, (New York: Plenum Press, 1981), pp. 1-71.
44. Anthony M. Orum, *Introduction to Political Sociology*. (Englewood Cliffs, N.J.: Princeton-Hall 1978).
45. Tom Bottomore:
    (i) *Elites and Society*. (London: Hutchinson & Co., 1964).
    (ii) *Political Sociology* (London: Hutchinson & Co., 1979).
46. S.N. Eisenstadt, *Modernization—Protest and Change*. (Englewood Cliffs, N.J.: Prentice-Hall 1966).
47. Cyril E. Black, *Dynamics of Modernization*. (New York: Harper & Row, 1966).
48. C. Wright Mills: *The Power Elite*. (New York: Oxford University Press, 1957).
49-50. Robert E. Dowse and John Hughes, *Political Sociology*. (London: John Wiley & Sons, 1972).
51. Morris Janowitz, 'Political Sociology' in David L. Sills (ed), *International Encyclopedia of Social Sciences*, Vol. 12. (New York: MacMillan & The Free Press, 1968), pp. 298-306.
52. Giovanni Sartori, 'From Sociology of Politics to Political Sociology', in S.M. Lipset (ed), *Politics and Social Sciences*. (New York: Oxford University Press, 1969), pp. 65-100.
53. *Ibid*., p. 92.
54. *Ibid*., p. 69.
55. *Ibid*., p. 69.
56. Leon H. Mayhew, 'Society' in David L. Sills (ed), *International Encyclopedia of Social Sciences*, Vol. 14. (New York: MacMillan & The Free Press, 1968), p. 577.
57. Talcott Parsons:
    (i) *Essays in Sociological Theory*. (Glencoe, Illinois: Free Press, 1948).
    (ii) *The Social System*. (Glencoe, Illinois: Free Press, 1951).
58. Gabriel A. Almond and Sidney Verba: *The Civic Culture*. (Princeton, N.J.: Princeton University Press, 4th Printing, 1972), p. 14.
59. David Easton, *The Political System: An Inquiry into the State of Political Science*. (Calcutta: Scientific Book Company, The Second Indian edition, 1971). p. 129.

60. Vernon Van Dyke, *Political Science: A Philosophical Analysis* (Stanford, California: Stanford University Press, 1962), p. 134. Originally published by the Stanford University Press in 1960.
61. Jean Blondel, *An Introduction to Comparative Government*. (London: Weidenfeld & Nicolson, 1969), p. 6.
62. Gabriel A. Almond and Sidney Verba, *The Civic Culture: Political Attitudes and Democracy in Five Nations*. (Princeton, N.J.: Princeton University Press, 4th Printing, 1972) p. 32. Originally Published by the Princeton University Press in 1963.
63. Tom Bottomore, *Political Sociology*. (New Delhi: B.I. Publications, First-Indian Edition, 1980), p. 7. Originally published by Hutchison & Co., London in 1979.
64. Giovanni Sartori, 'From Sociology of Politics to Political Sociology' in S.M. Lipset (ed), *Politics and The Social Sciences*. (New York: Oxford University Press, 1969), p. 69.
65. Morris Janowitz, 'Political Sociology' in David L. Sills (ed), *International Encyclopedia of Social Sciences*, Vol. 12. (New York: Macmillan and the Free Press, 1968), pp. 298-299.
66. Richard G. Braungart, 'Political Sociology' in Samuel Long (ed), *The Handbook of Political Behaviour*, Vol. 3 (New York: Plenum Press, 1981), p. 3.
67. Michael Rush and Philip Althoff, *An Introduction to Political Sociology* (London: Thomas Nelson & Sons, 1971), p. 3.
68. Robert E. Dowse and John A. Hughes, *Political Sociology*. (London: John Wiley & Sons, 1972), p. 7.
69. *Ibid*., p. 13.
70. *Ibid*., p. 9.
71. *Ibid*., p. 9.
72. Anthony M. Orum, Introduction to Political Sociology. (Englewood Cliffs, N.J.: Prentice-Hall, 1978), p. 1.
73. Tom Bottomore, Political Sociology. (Indian Edition), *op. cit.*, p. 8.
74. Reinhard Bendix and S.M. Lipset, 'Political Sociology—An Essay and Bibliography', in Current Sociology (Paris: UNESCO, 1957), p. 57.
75. Lewis A. Coser (ed.), *Political Sociology*. (New York: Harper & Row 1966), p. 1.
76. Samuel Greer and Peter Orleans, 'Political Sociology' in R.L. Faris (ed). *Handbook of Modern Sociology*. *Op. cit.* p. 808.
77. *Ibid*. p. 810.
78. Giovanni Sartori, 'From Sociology of Politics to Political Sociology' in S.M. Lipset (ed), *Politics and The Social Sciences*. *Op. cit.*, p. 69.
79. *Ibid*., p. 69.

80. S.M. Lipset: 'Political Sociology' in Neil J. Smelsor (ed), *Sociology: An Introduction* (New Delhi: Wiley Eastern, 1967).
81. Richard G. Braungart, 'Political Sociology' in Samuel Long (ed), *The Handbook of Political Behaviour*, Vol. 3, *op. cit.*, p. 7.
82. Giovani Sartori: 'From Sociology of Politics to Political Sociology' in S.M. Lipset (ed), *Politics and the Social Sciences*, *op. cit.*, p. 89. Also, S.M. Lipset and S. Rokkan (eds), *Party Systems and Vote Alignments*. (New York: Free Press, 1967), pp. 26-33.
83. Maurice Duverger (ed): *The Study of Politics*. Translated by Robert Wagoner (London: Nelson, 1972), p. 11.
84. H.V. Wiseman: Politics: *The Master Science*. (London: Routledge and Kegan Paul, 1969 p. 35.

2

A Framework for Analysis

2.1 A Liberal-Democratic Framework

For the study and analysis of interactions between Society and Politics, scholars may design and employ various frameworks and approaches. In this context, however, due care must be taken in designing and employing the most relevant framework and approach especially in view of the scope of Political Sociology that focuses on interpenetration, reciprocal influences, and freedom of interactions between Society and Politics. Since, the scope of Political Sociology is different from that of Sociology of Politics, the frameworks and approaches that pertain to the latter seems to be irrelevant to the former. As such, pure sociological approaches of Max Weber and other Sociologists as well as economic approaches of Karl Marx and other Marxian scholars that consider sociological or economic factor as the only explanatory variable and determinant of Politics, and that focus exclusively on the study of the influence of Society on Politics, not the *viceversa*, are lopsided, incomplete, and prejudiced in undertaking a balanced and holistic study of "Society-Politics Interactions". Hence, in view of the nature and scope of Political Sociology, pure sociological and Marxian frameworks and approaches seem to be academically unhelpful and incomplete for the study of the "two-way process" of interactions between Society and Politics. On the contrary, the liberal-democratic frameworks and approaches designed to study "Open Society-Polity Interactions" seem to be most suited for the analysis of reciprocal influences between sociological and political phenomena. In this context, academically, the most relevant framework for the study of "Society-Politics Interactions" seems to be the "Theory of Political System".

This conceptual framework is founded on the assumption that the Political System is the system of politics of a National Society; and that it interacts with the latter on the basis of the principles of openness, self-operation, and self-regulation[1]. The Political System which is an integral part of the Society interacts with the latter openly in the sense that it is susceptible to societal influences, and it responds to these influences. The Society, as a whole, tends to influence the people to form demands on varieties of societal issues, and these demands are transmitted to the Political System for enacting authoritative decisions and policies. On receiving the demands and support of the people, what may be termed as "Inputs", the Political System processes these on functioning as a self-operating system, and produces authoritative decisions in the form of laws, rules, regulations, and public policies, what may be termed as "Outputs". As and when the 'outputs' are implemented, people form opinions on these, what may be termed as "Feedback Information", which are re-processed by the Political System into fresh "Outputs". Therefore, the Political System tends to function as a self-regulating system in correcting itself or changing its 'outputs' in conformity with the people's opinions as necessitated for its very survival. Thus, in this over-all process of interactions, the Society tends to influence the Political System through "Inputs" that are generated as a consequence of societal influences, and simultaneously, the Political System, through "outputs" as produced by it, tends to influence the Society.

The "Theory of Political System", is, thus, a conceptual framework which is founded on the basic assumption of freedom of interactions and reciprocal influences between the Society and the Polity. As such, it seems to be the most relevant and meaningful framework for undertaking the study and analysis of "Society-Politics Interactions."

In conceptualizing it, credit goes to two great Political Sociologists such as David Easton[2] and Gabriel A. Almond[3] who view it in different perspectives and have designed different models.

2.2 Easton's Model of Political System

David Easton defines Political System as "a set of interactions, abstracted from the totality of social behaviour, through which values are authoritatively allocated for a society"[4]. According to him, the Political System is constituted of the mass of political behaviour, activities and roles undertaken by the people of a National Society in the context of authoritative allocation of values for it. Hence, the distinguishing attribute of the Political System is its exclusive concern for, and involvement with "authoritative allocation of values" for the Society on facilitating the performance of relevant activities and roles by its people. Therefore, the Political System survives as long as it is able to perform successfully the task of authoritative allocation of values for the Society. For this purpose, the Political System is required to retain constantly, through time, two essential variables[5] or life-conditions such as: (i) the capacity to allocate values for the Society through an allocative apparatus, and (ii) the capacity to get these allocations accepted as 'authoritative' or 'binding' by most of the people in most of the time. Successful retention of these two life-conditions enables the Political System to persist through time.

In other words, it may be said to persist, and its life-process may be said to continue as long as it is able to allocate values, and it is able to get these allocations accepted as authoritative by people as well. Therefore, the essential concern or the ultimate goal of the Political System is "Persistence" which it strives to attain and retain in the process of its interactions with the 'environment' as an "Input-output Mechanism". Its dynamics may be illustrated by a simplified diagram of Easton's Model of the Political System (*see* Fig. 2.1).

The Political System of a National Society exists and operates in a comprehensive environment that includes both the "Intra-Societal Environment" and the "Extra-Societal Envronment"[6]. The" Intra-Societal Environment" consists of all systems of the National Society such as its ecological system, biological system, personality system, social system, cultural system, economic system, demographic system etc; whereas the "Extra-Societal Environment" consist of all systems of the International Society such as its international political system, international ecological system, international social system, international economic system, international demographic system etc.

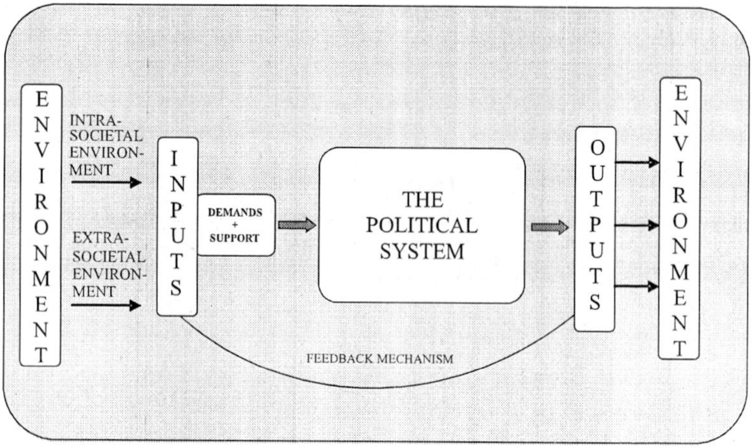

A Simplified Diagram of Easton's Model of the Political System[7]

Thus, all systems of the National Society, and all systems of the International Society, taken together, constitute the totality of the Environment within which the National Political System exists, and operates in a state of constant interactions with it. The Environment, as a whole, tends to influence the people of the National Society in the context of formation of demands on varieties of issues. A demand may be defined as 'an expression of the opinion that an authoritative allocation with regard to a particular subject matter should or should not be made by those responsible for doing so"[8], and it may originate as a consequence of the impact of the "Environment". For instance, inflation, a domestic economic phenomenon, may induce the people to make demands upon the Authority of the Political System to enact suitable laws and regulations to stabilize the prices of essential commodities, and to make them available through public shops at fair prices. Similarly, the Universal declaration of Human Rights of the UN, an international political phenomenon, may induce the people to make demands for enacting suitable laws for protecting and promoting Human Rights, and for instituting the National Human Rights Commission. Thus, both 'Intra-societal Environment' and 'Extra-societal Environment' may influence the people to make demands for authoritative allocation and decisions on varieties of issues that interest them in the domestic and the international arenas. The processing of these demands, however, requires support that may be defined as favourable orientations and actions[9] of the people towards their political system. Support may, therefore, be of two types[10] such as: (i) covert support when it takes the form of favourable feelings, sentiments and attitude, and (ii) overt support when it takes the form of favourable activities and behaviour.

People may form and display support towards the National Political System in respect of its three major objects such as, the Political Community, the Regime, and the Authorities.[11] The Political Community refers to the total body of members of the Political System seen as "a group of persons bound together by a political division of labour for attainment of common political objectives through a common structure and set of processes"[12]; the Regime connotes the Constitutional Order[13] including values (goals), norms (principles), and structure of Authority (patterns of distribution of legitimate power) that provide the framework for political interactions, and for making of authoritative decisions; whereas the Authorities are those persons who are incumbents[14] or occupants of the decision-making structure, for instance the members of the legislature or the executive, and who are, thus, entrusted with the task of making of authoritative decisions at a given point of time. These political objects become the objects of support when people are favourably oriented towards them. Their support towards the Political System, as a whole, on being combined with their demands on varieties of issues facilitates formation of "Inputs"[15].

'Inputs', thus formed, are fed into the Political System in which these are processed by the 'Authorities' in conformity with the 'Regime'(Constitutional provisions), and as a consequence, there are produced 'Outputs' or authoritative decisions in the form of laws, rules, regulations, and public policies. These 'Outputs', produced in response to the 'inputs', are disseminated into the 'environment', and are implemented on the people who, as a consequence, form and ventilate opinions and reactions toward them. People may view the 'outputs' with favour or disfavour, and thus, their, positive opinions or negative reactions constitute 'Feedback Information' which are again fed into the Political System as fresh 'inputs' through the "Feedback Mechanisms" for producing new or reformed 'outputs' by the 'Authorities'.

The 'positive' feedback information and opinions encourage the

Authorities to continue with the original output; whereas the 'negative' feedback information and reactions provide opportunities to them to adjust or change the original outputs in conformity with the opinions of the people for obtaining their support for the Political System. Thus, Easton portrays "A Dynamic Response Model of Political System"[16] that is embedded in a wide environment, and that too, is in a state of regular interactions with it. The environment, on facilitating the genesis of "inputs", tends to influence the dynamics of the Political System which, in turn, through "outputs" produced by it, tends to influence the environment. These interactions and interrelationships are cyclical, and these tend to enliven the Political System in the context of attainment of the goal of 'Systemic-persistence'.

2.2.1 Stresses

The Political System, however, is susceptible to environmental challenges because of its openness. The Environment may influence and facilitate formation of such inputs that may challenge the life-conditions of the Political System, and consequently, its persistence, in the sense of its ability to allocate values and its ability to get the allocations accepted as authoritative by the people, may be lost or undermined. These environmental challenges that take the form of detrimental inputs are termed as 'Stresses'[17]. As "Inputs" consist of both demands and support, there may be discerned two major types of stresses such as "Demand-stress", and "Support-stress". When demands that flow into the Political System tend to challenge and endanger its allocative ability to produce outputs, the stress experienced by it because of demand-overload may be termed as 'Demand-Stress'.[18] It may occur if the Political System is overloaded with demands in respect of both quantity and quality.

When the Political System encounters a huge number of demands, and experiences difficulties to process these within a specified time-span available to it, the stress experienced by it because of quantitative excess of demands may be termed as 'Volume-Stress'[19]; whereas the difficulties experienced by the Political System to process such demands that lack in general consensus, create substantive contention among the people, challenge its normative framework, and hence, require more time for processing because of qualitative excess, may be termed as 'Content-Stress'[20]. These types of demand-stresses tend to affect adversely the ability of the Political System to allocate values.

Besides demand-stresses involving both volume-stress and content-stress, the Political System may experience 'Support-Stress'[21] caused by loss or decline and erosion of support of the people, below a minimal level, for each of the three major political objects such as the Political Community, the Regime, and the Authorities. Support-stress may be experienced at the level of the 'Political Community' if there emerges widespread and irreconcilable dissensions among the people as to a common pattern of political life and existence. For instance, when different sections of the population desire for divergent patterns of political life such as Parliamentary democracy, Presidential Democracy, Communism, Monarchy, Dictatorship etc., and no consensus is arrived at, the unity and integration of the Political Community becomes endangered. 'Support-stress' may also become evident at the level of the 'Regime', when a large majority of people refuses to respect and obey the Constitutional Order. Similarly, when people refuse to legitimize the outputs produced by the 'Authorities' at a given point of time, and as a consequence, it becomes difficult to implement the 'outputs' effectively, it may be inferred that 'support-stress' has emerged at the level of the 'Authorities'.

Thus, the Political System may experience loss, decline or erosion of support of the people at the level of each of the three major political objects such as the Political Community, the Regime, and the Authorities. These support-stresses may adversely affect the ability of the Political System to get its allocations accepted as authoritative by the people; and without their support, it experiences difficulties in implementing its outputs effectively.

Thus, varieties of demand-stresses and support-stresses may endanger but not necessarily destroy completely the ability of the Political System to allocate values, and also its ability to get these allocations accepted as authoritative by its people. In these stressful situations, no doubt, the Political System may find it difficult to discharge its basic functions smoothly, and to realize the ultimate goal of persistence successfully. However, stresses may become intolerable for the Political System when its essential variables or 'life-conditions' are sought to be completely destroyed, and the prospect of its persistence becomes minimal. Such a stressful condition in which the entropy of the Political System seems to be imminent may be termed as 'Critical Range'[22].

2.2.2 Stress-Regulation Mechanisms

When stressful conditions affect adversely the essential variables or life conditions of the Political System, and consequently its survival or persistence seems to be at stake, it tends to regulate and reduce stresses in order to keep them within tolerable limit as deemed necessary for continuance of its life-process. For regulation of demand-stresses, the Political System may take the help of some important devices or mechanisms such as 'Structural Mechanisms', 'Cultural Mechanisms', 'Communication Mechanisms', and 'Reduction Mechanisms'[23].

In the process of formation of demands on varieties of societal issues, crucial roles may be played by some 'structural mechanisms'[24] such as pressure groups, political parties, mass-media, opinion-leaders, and the elites. These structures or agencies not only articulate and aggregate the demands but also facilitate their entry into the Political System for conversion into authoritative decisions. Hence, on acting as "Gate-keepers", they may regulate the flow of demands in terms of volume and content, and may protect the Political System from the adverse effects of demand-stresses. Besides structural mechanisms, the societal culture and its norms and values may serve as effective 'cultural mechanisms'[25] in regulating the volume and content of demands. For instance, if the values of peaceful co-existence, religious tolerance and secularism characterize the culture of the people of a Society, these cultural values as cherished and practiced by various social groups, may refrain and restrain the people from making demands for instituting 'state-religion', and creating communal disharmony. Thus, the Political System may be protected against demand-stresses through cultural regulation of demands.

Demand-Stresses may also be regulated by the 'communication mechanisms'[26]. For this purpose, structures such as pressure-groups, political parties, legislature, executive, judiciary and the mass-media may also work as communication channels in transmitting relevant political information to the people for attainment of the goal 'systemic persistence'. Thus, the communication mechanisms may undertake political education of the people so that they would refrain themselves from making deviant and irrelevant demands, and the Political System is insulated from demand-stresses.

Besides the communication mechanisms, the Political System, for coping with demand-stresses, may also take the help of the 'reduction mechanisms'[27] such as pressure-groups, political parties, and legislature which serve to reduce demand-overload on combining and aggregating identical, similar, or compatible demands into a few alternative policy-proposals, and also facilitating the smooth conversion of the proposed policy-alternatives into authoritative decisions. For instance, demands on medical care, appointment and salary of doctors, production of medicines, health insurance etc. may be aggregated under health-issue, and be converted into health-policy. This process of reduction of the number of demands through combination and aggregation may facilitate regulation of demand-stresses in terms of both volume and content.

As regard support-stress caused due to loss, erosion or decline of support of the people towards the Political System, the latter is required to generate and foster a generalized attachment, what Easton terms as "Diffuse Support"[28], towards its political objects such as "the Political Community, the Regime, and the Authorities" for realizing the goal of "systemic persistence". It is "a reservoir of favourable attitudes or good will"[29] of the people, without any expectation of direct or specific benefits, that helps them "to accept or tolerate outputs to which they are opposed or the effect of which they see as damaging to their wants"[30]. Diffuse Support is, therefore, a minimal level of support that enables the Political System to get its outputs accepted as legitimate by the people, and consequently, to persist through time. It may be formed in the people through the process of "Political Socialization"[31] involving the inculcation of a sense of legitimacy[32] towards the Regime, and the Authorities, and also a sense of identity[33] toward the Political Community.

Apart from generating 'diffuse-support' through the process of 'political socialization' as a long-term measure, the Political System may recruit specific support for its political objects such as the Authorities, the Regime, and the Political Community on producing 'outputs' in satisfaction to the demands of the people, or changing the outputs, and even its "Authority-structure" and the "Regime" in conformity with the people's negative feedback information so that the people would become satisfied, and support it[34].

Thus, the Political System may undertake endeavours, through various stress-regulation mechanisms and measures, in order to cope with both demand-stress and support-stress. Consequently, it may be enabled to allocate values for the Society, and also, to get these allocations accepted as authoritative by its people through time. In the process, if so required by the demands of its people, it may change its norms as well as forms, radically and frequently, for attaining the goal of "systemic-persistence".

2.3 Almond's Model of Political System

Almond defines Political System as "that system of interactions to be found in all independent societies which performs the functions of integration and adaptation (both internally and *vis-à-vis* other societies) by means of the employment, or threat of employment, of more or less legitimate physical compulsion".[35]

According to him, the Political System, in the context of its working as an "Input-Output Mechanism", always strives to keep itself integrated on suitably adapting with both the intra-societal environment and the extra-societal environment. Its prime concern is maintenance of its form and norms (its structural arrangement and the corresponding cultural pattern) intact, if necessary, on the employment of legitimate physical power through its armed forces. Thus, its dynamics, in the context of formation of both 'Inputs' and 'Outputs' for attainment of the ultimate goal of "systemic-maintenance" involves, directly or indirectly, employment of legitimate physical power. Therefore, Almond conceptualizes the Political System essentially in system-maintenance perspective, and considers it as a system of behaviour related to the inter-play of legitimate power for the attainment of the goal of 'systemic-maintenance'.

As a system of political behaviour, it constantly interacts with the environment, and produces "Outputs" in response to "Inputs" so as to maintain, intact, its structural arrangement and the congruent pattern of political culture through time. Its dynamics may be illustrated by the following diagram drawn in conformity with Almond's conceptualization.

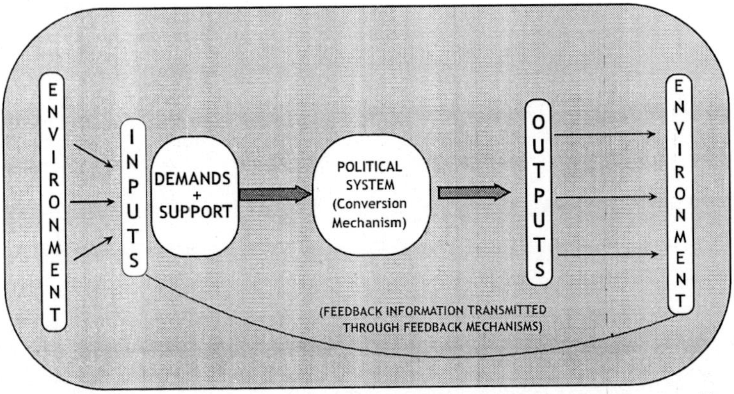

A Simplified Diagram of Almond's Model of Political System[36]

The wide environment consisting of both the National Society and the International Society influences the people in the context of formation of demands on varieties of societal issues, and also in the context of genesis of their support towards their Political System. Their demands and support taken together constitute "Inputs" which are transmitted to the Political System for conversion into "Outputs". According to Almond, demands may be classified into four broad categories[37] such as: (i) demands for allocation of goods and services, for instance, demands for wages and salaries, educational opportunities, health services, employment in pubic services (both civil and military) etc., (ii) demands for regulation of behaviour, for instance, demands for provisions for safety and security of life, control over market etc.; (iii) demands for participation in the Political System, for instance, demands for the right of voting, to contest at the elections and to hold public offices, to organize political associations and parties etc.; and (iv) demands for communication and information, for instance, demands for the right to be informed of governmental decisions and public policies, demands for the right to own and operate media of communication etc. All these demands may be combined in various forms and degrees of intensity.

Apart from demands, the other component of "Input" is support which may be classified into four major types[38] such as: (i) material support, for instance, payment of taxes and other levies, rendering public services, both civil and military etc.; (ii) behavioural support, for instance, rendering obedience to laws and regulations;

(iii) participatory support, for instance, voting at the elections, rendering other forms of political activities in support of the Political System etc.; and (iv) moral support, for instance, payment of deference or respect to public authorities, symbols and ceremonials of the Political System. All these various types of support may be combined with above mentioned kinds of demands in variety of ways as well as degrees of intensity for constituting "Inputs".

The "Inputs" thus formed are processed by the Political System which converts them into "Outputs" or authoritative decisions. The outputs produced by the Political System may also be classified into four major types[39] such as: (i) extractive outputs, for instance, taxes and levies to be paid by the people; and public services, both civil and military to be rendered by them; (ii) regulative outputs, for instance, laws, rules and regulations enacted for regulating behaviour of the people for maintenance of public order, safety and security of the National Society, and protection of rights of the people; (iii) distributive outputs, for instance, authoritative decisions made for allocation of public goods and services among the people; and (iv) symbolic outputs, for instance, laws and regulations enacted for honouring symbols and ceremonials of the Political System.

2.3.1 Structural-Functional Analysis

Thus, according to Almond, the Political System essentially works as a conversion mechanism for converting "Inputs" into "Outputs", of course on being always alert and attentive to the attainment of the goal of 'systemic-maintenance'. Hence, "Conversion Function" is the first and the most fundamental function[40] of the Political System. However, the conversion process through which inputs are converted into outputs involves performance of six different types[41] of functions such as interest-articulation, interest-aggregation, rule-making, rule-application, rule-adjudication, and political-communication.

The function of interest-articulation is the first functional step that initiates the System's conversion process, and activates it. The interests or preferences of the people on varieties of societal issues take the form of demands which are articulated and organized by interest-groups and pressure-groups such as racial and ethnic groups, caste and tribal groups, language and religious groups, occupational groups etc. Every group cherishes and champions a distinct interest, and works for its attainment on influencing the Authority or Government of the Political System. The articulated interests of these various groups, on the basis of their compatibility and interrelatedness, are sought to the aggregated and harmoniously combined by political parties, and are presented as alternative policy-proposals or party-manifestos. Thus, when the function of interest-articulation is performed by pressure-groups, and the function of interest-aggregation is performed by political parties, "Inputs" take concrete shape, and these are fed into the Political System in which the Authority or Government, working as "Conversion-Mechanism", converts the inputs into outputs. This function of converting inputs into outputs is essentially performed by the legislature that makes authoritative decisions in the form of laws, rules, regulations, and public policies in response to the incoming inputs. As and when, the legislature makes laws, rules, and public-policies, these are implemented and enforced by the executive and the bureaucracy. However, there emerges the need for scrutiny of the laws as made by the legislature, and implemented by the executive for ascertaining as to whether these conform to the provisions of the Constitution. The scrutiny of legislative and executive actions, and their adjudication are undertaken by the judiciary. Thus, the governmental structures such as the legislature, the executive, and the judiciary are essentially concerned with the performance of the functions of rule-making, rule-application, and rule-adjudication respectively.

However, in the process of conversion of 'inputs' into 'outputs', the performance of the above-mentioned functions by their corresponding specialized structures tends to be crucially dependent upon the performance of the political communication function[42] that involves free flow of political information from the environment to the Political System and *viceversa*, and also within the Political System from one structure to another[43]. Without true, relevant, and adequate political information comprising demands and decisions, it may not be feasible to perform the functions of interest-articulation, interest-aggregation, rule-making, rule-application, and rule adjudication meaningfully by their corresponding specialized structures. Therefore, the function of political-communication may be likened to the function of circulation of blood in the body-politic; and the structures which specialize in it are the mass-media.

Thus, the Political System is enabled to convert 'inputs' into 'outputs' as and when all conversion functions are performed by their corresponding structures. However, emergence of distinct structures that specialize in the performance of their corresponding conversion functions is the hallmark of a developed Political System.

Besides the "Conversion Function", the second major category of function of the Political System comprises the functions of "System-maintenance and Adaptation"[44], which are termed by Almond as the functions of "Political Socialization and Recruitment"[45]. Like a system in general, the survival and continuing existence of the Political System tends to be crucially dependent upon its ability to maintain itself, and also to adapt itself with the environment. For this purpose, it constantly performs the function of political-recruitment as well as the function of political socialization.

In this context, recruitment and appointment of persons and personnel are made continuously for its various structures such as pressure groups, parties, legislature, executive, judiciary, and mass-media so that these structures are enabled to perform their corresponding functions, and the Political System as a whole becomes dynamic and enlivened. However, survival of the Political System, in the sense of maintenance of its form or structural arrangement intact, tends to be dependent upon successful socialization of the personnel of the various structures as well as the people of the Society as a whole in the congruent and allegiant pattern of political culture that would help sustain and nourish it. For instance, the "Civic Culture" is the congruent pattern of political culture for a democratic form of Political System, and for maintaining and sustaining it, its people need to be socialized in the "Civic Culture". Hence, the Political System, through varieties of political socialization-agencies such as family, school and educational institutions, peer-group, mass-media, political parties, secondary groups, governmental institutions, and the political process, continuously performs the function of political socialization so as to generate and foster supportive psychology and behaviour in the people towards it. Therefore, the function of political socialization and recruitment is as important as the conversion function; and all these functions are required to be performed in such a way as to enable the Political System to attain the goal of 'systemic-maintenance' through time.

Thus, according to Almond, every Political System performs, on the whole, seven kinds[46] of different functions such as the functions of political socialization and recruitment, political communication, interest-articulation, interest-aggregation, rule-making, rule-application, and rule-adjudication by its structures. Therefore, all Political Systems are characterized by "universality of political functions",[47] and also "universality of political structures"[48]. However, different patterns of "structural-functional relationship"[49] may characterize them; and hence, the status and rank of each Political System in the modern-traditional continuum may be ascertained on the basis of the analysis of the prevailing pattern of "structural-functional relationship". According to Almond, the major attributes of a modern and developed Political System are: (i) a high degree of structural-differentiation, and (ii) a high degree of functional specificity cum specialization.[50] In this context 'structural-differentiation" connotes formation of all political infrastructures such as interest and pressure-groups, political parties, mass-media, agencies of political socialization and recruitment, legislature, executive, and judiciary, and each of these must have its own distinct identity, autonomy, and be different from the other's structures; whereas 'functional-specificity-cum-specialization' requires that every structure shall perform its specific function and specialize in it, as for instance, the specific functions for pressure-group, political party, legislature, executive, judiciary, mass-media, agencies political socialization and recruitment are respectively the functions of interest—articulation, interest-aggregation, rule-making, rule-application, rule-adjudication, political-communication, and political socialization and recruitment. Therefore, the greater the degree of structural-differentiation and functional-specificity-cum-specialization in a Political System, the higher may be the relative level of its modernity and development. Thus, for becoming dynamic, the Political System is required to perform all its functions by the corresponding structures. However, in view of the dynamics of the Political System as an "Input-Output Mechanism", there may be discerned two major functional categories[51] such as: (i) 'Input-functions' that include the functions of political socialization and recruitment, political-communication, interest-articulation, and interest-aggregation; and (ii) 'Output-functions' that include the functions of rule-making, rule-application, and rule-adjudication. The effective performance of these 'input' and 'output' functions by the corresponding structures enables the Political System to process and convert "Inputs" into "Outputs", and also to maintain itself in tact through time.

2.3.2 Systemic Capability

On the whole, the Political System constantly interacts with its environment and strives incessantly to realize the basic objective of "systemic-maintenance". In this context, the 'outputs' produced by it in response to the 'inputs' reveal its capability which is defined by Almond as its "over-all performance as a unit in its environment"[52]. System's capability may be empirically discerned, and classified into four broad categories such as: (i) extractive capability, (ii) regulative capability, (iii) distributive capability, and (iv) responsive capability.[53] Extractive capability refers to the extent and range of the System's ability to draw material and human resources from its people in the form of taxes, levies, and services. Regulative capability connotes the scope and intensity of the System's ability to regulate and control behaviour of its people so as to maintain peace and order in the Society, and to protect their legitimate interests and rights in inter-individual relationships. Distributive capability refers to the range of the System's ability to allocate and distribute, among the people, goods and services available at its disposal on enacting and implementing welfare public-policies. Responsive-capability connotes the extent of the System's ability to respond to people's demands and opinions, and to become responsible and responsive to them.

It is, of course, the responsive capability[53] which tends to determine crucially all other capabilities of the System because it facilitates legitimization of the Political System on forming, fostering, and reinforcing support and allegiance towards it. Consequently, people are motivated to pay taxes, render public-services, and to abide by laws and rules with spontaneity and sincerity; and hence the System is enabled to display high extractive, regulative and distributive capabilities.

All these types of capabilities of the Political System are, indeed, patterns of its performance as a unit in its environment in the context of flow of inputs into it, and production of outputs by it. However, the Political System is required to form, and adjust it capabilities in such a way so as to attain the basic ultimate goal of "systemic-maintenance" through time. Moreover, the Political System is required to form and display all its capabilities in a higher degree so that it may attain a relatively more developed and modern status.[55] Thus, Almond conceptualizes a model of Political System in both systemic-maintenance and political development perspectives.

2.4 Need for Synthesis

Thus, both Easton and Almond employ the 'Systems-Theory' in analyzing political life in relation to the Society, and have conceptualized models of Political System for understanding and explaining the dynamics of the Political Society. However, their perspectives are different and divergent. Whereas Easton conceptualizes the Political System in "systemic-persistence" perspective, Almond constructs his model in "systemic-maintenance" perspective.

The "systemic-persistence" model of Easton focuses exclusively on the System's survival on retaining two life-conditions or essential variables such as its ability to allocate values or make decisions, and its ability to get these allocations accepted as legitimate by the people, but it is unconcerned with vital political changes that may take place in its norms and form. Rather, it allows for fundamental changes, if necessary, in the structure and culture of the Political System so as to persist through time. Easton's model is, therefore, unconcerned with the need for political stability in the sense of stability of the prevalent form of the Political System. On the contrary, Almond's "systemic-maintenance" model focuses exclusively on the retention of the prevalent structure and culture of the Political System intact, and does not allow fundamental changes in its norms and form. Almonds' model is, therefore, unconcerned with the inevitability of political change. Thus, neither Easton's model nor Almond's model seems to conform to the real-world situations because every actual Political System strives for political stability, and it is also a fact that no actual Political System can maintain its culture and structure intact without bringing about political changes, if necessary, in its norms and form. Therefore, for designing a realistic and meaningful conceptual framework for the study of the dynamics of the Political Society on enquiring into, and analyzing the interactions between Society and Politics, it seems necessary to combine or synthesize the perspectives, approaches, and models of Political System of both Easton and Almond.

REFERENCES

1. (i) David Easton: "An Approach to the Analysis of Political System", *World Politics*, Vol. IX, No. 3, (April 1957) pp. 383-399.
   (ii) Gabriel A. Almond: "An Introduction: A Functional Approach to Comparative Politics" in Gabriel A. Almond and James S. Coleman (eds), *The Politics of Developing Areas*. (Princeton, N.J.: Princeton University Press, 1960), Paperback Edition, 1970. p. 7.
2. David Easton:
   (i) *A Framework for Political Analysis*. (Englewood Cliffs, N.J.: Prentice-Hall, 1965).
   (ii) *A Systems Analysis of Political Life*. (New York: John Wiley & Sons, 1965).
3. Gabriel A. Almond:
   (i) *The Politics of Developing Areas*. Edited with James S. Coleman, *op. cit.*
   (ii) *Comparative Politics: A Developmental Approach* (Boston: Little, Brown & Co. 1966) in collaboration with G.B. Powell, Jr.
4. David Easton: A Framework for Political Analysis. *Op. cit.* p. 57.
5. *Ibid.*, p. 96. Also, David Easton: *A Systems Analysis of Political Life*. *Op. cit.*, p. 24.
6. David Easton: *A Systems Analysis of Political Life*. *Op. cit.*, p. 32.
7. *Ibid.*, p. 21.
8. *Ibid.*, p. 38.
9. *Ibid.*, p. 159.
10. *Ibid.*, pp. 159-160.
11. *Ibid.*, p. 165.
12. *Ibid.*, p. 177.
13. *Ibid.*, p. 179.
14. *Ibid.*, p. 212.
15. *Ibid.*, p. 29.
16. *Ibid.*, p. 30.
17. *Ibid.*, p. 33.
18. *Ibid.*, p. 57.
19. *Ibid.*, p. 59.
20. *Ibid.*, p. 59.
21. *Ibid.*, pp. 156, 157, 220.

22. David Easton: *A Framework for Political Analysis. Op. cit.*, p. 93.
23. David Easton: *A Systems Analysis of Political Life. Op. cit.*, pp. 85-149.
24. *Ibid.*, p. 85.
25. *Ibid.*, p. 100.
26. *Ibid.*, p. 117.
27. *Ibid.*, p. 128.
28. *Ibid.*, pp. 272-273.
29. *Ibid.*, p. 273.
30. *Ibid.*, p. 273.
31. *Ibid.*, p. 301.
32. *Ibid.*, p. 278.
33. *Ibid.*, p. 325.
34. *Ibid.*, pp. 247-249, 343-347.
35. Gabriel A. Almond: "Introduction: A Functional Approach to Comparative Politics", in Gabriel A. Almond and James S. Coleman (eds), *The Politics of Developing Areas*. (Princeton, N.J.: Princeton University Press, Paperback Edn., 1970), p. 7.
36. Gabriel A. Almond and G.B. Powell, Jr: *Comparative Politics: A Developmental Approach*. (New Delhi: Amerind Publishing Co, Indian Reprint, 1975) pp. 20-21, Originally published by Little, Brown & Co Boston, U.S.A. in 1966.
37. *Ibid.*, p. 25.
38. *Ibid.*, p. 26.
39. *Ibid.*, p. 27.
40. *Ibid.*, p. 29.
41. *Ibid.*, p. 29.
42. *Ibid.*, p. 166.
43. *Ibid.*, p. 29.
44. *Ibid.*, p. 29.
45. *Ibid.*, p. 30.
46. Gabriel A. Almond: "Introduction: A Functional Approach to Comparative Politics", *op. cit.* p. 17.
47. *Ibid.*, p. 12.
48. *Ibid.*, p. 11.
49. *Ibid.*, p. 11.
50. *Ibid.*, p. 11, p. 18.
51. *Ibid.*, p. 17.
52. Gabriel A. Almond: *Comparative Politics: A developmental Approach*, *op. cit.* p. 28.
53. *Ibid.*, p. 29.
54. *Ibid.*, p. 201.
55. *Ibid.*, p. 38, 207.

3

Influence, Power, and Authority

Politics being defined as "authoritative allocation of values for a society"[1], the dynamics of the 'Political Society' and its socio-political process revolve round the institution of 'Authority'. However, 'Authority' is a kind of 'Power'[2], and 'Power' is a kind of 'Influence'[3] even though these three terms do not connote the same meaning. However, an analysis of these three inter-related phenomena seems imperative for undertaking a realistic study of the socio-political process.

3.1 Influence

The term 'Influence' connotes the ability of an actor to bring about desired changes in the behaviour or policies of another actor or actors on persuading them. Scholars have defined it in various ways, yet the definition given by Robert A. Dahl seems to be the most succinct one, and hence, it may be adopted for understanding the phenomenon of "Influence". Dahl defines: "Influence is a relation among actors in which one actor induces other actors to act in some way they would not otherwise act."[4] This definition given by Dahl clearly focuses on the following distinguishing attributes of the phenomenon of Influence:

(i) Basically, 'Influence' is an inter-personal relationship between two (at the minimum) or more actors; and the actors may be individuals, groups, societies, and even states.
(ii) In this relationship, one actor induces (persuades) another

actor or actors to change their behaviour in conformity with his desire and directions. The term 'behaviour' is a broad one that includes overt-activities, policies, pre-disposition, beliefs and values, and it involves changes as desired by the former. For the purpose of conceptual clarity, let us illustrate this relationship between two symbolic actors such as 'A' and 'B' as follows:

'A' does not influence, B does 'X'. (original behaviour of 'B')

When A influences, B ceases to do 'X', and does 'Y' (subsequent behaviour as desired by 'A').

In this illustration, no relationship of influence prevails between 'A' and 'B' so long as 'A' does not undertake endeavours, intentionally and successfully, to bring about desired changes in 'B's behaviour. Hence, it may be termed as a situation of 'non-influence' because 'B' performs his original activity or behaviour 'X' with complete freedom. But, when 'A' exercises influence against 'B', the latter ceases to do 'X' (the original behaviour) because of loss of freedom, and does 'Y' (the subsequent behaviour) as desired and directed by 'A'. This change in B's behaviour from 'X' to 'Y' takes place because 'B' is induced by 'A' to do so. The act inducement undertaken by 'A' entails loss of freedom of 'B', and brings about desired changes in the latter's behaviour. Therefore, the act of inducement is, indeed, the act of influence, and its use paves for the prevalence of an 'influence-relationship' between 'A' and 'B' entailing changes in 'B's behaviour as desired and directed by 'A'.

Thus, the phenomenon of 'Influence' involves a relationship between the 'Influencer' and the 'Influencee'. In this relationship, the 'influencer' is able to bring about desired changes in the behaviour of the 'influencee' on performing the act of inducement or persuasion which, of course, necessitates possession and skilful utilization of vital resources such as wealth, social status, knowledge and expertise, charisma etc. As Lasswell and Kaplan point out: "To have influence is to occupy a high position with respect to all the values important in the society"[5]. Moreover, it is required that the resources must be intentionally and skilfully exploited by the 'influencer' for persuading the 'influencee' to comply with his desires and directions. Hence, mere possession of resources without an intention to exploit these skilfully for bringing about desired changes in others' behaviour may endow an actor with the capacity for potential influence but would not make him an 'influencer' in reality. For instance, when a teacher intentionally instructs the students in the class-room to read the books as prescribed by him, and the latter on being persuaded by the teacher change their reading behaviour as desired by the former, a relationship of influence is established between the teacher and the students. On the contrary, if the teacher while teaching the students in the class-room does not intentionally and skilfully use his resource (knowledge) to induce or persuade the students to change their reading behaviour, it may be inferred that the teacher is not an 'influencer' in his relationship with the students, and that there prevails no relationship of influence between the teacher and the students in this context. Therefore, the three prerequisites for exercising actual influence by the 'influencer' are: (i) resources, (ii) intention, and (iii) skill for exploiting the resources in order to bring about desired changes in the behaviour of the 'influencee'.

Thus, 'influence-relationship' involves act of inducement or persuasion undertaken by the 'influencer' against the 'influencee', and simultaneously, compliance by the 'influencee' to the intention of the 'influencer'. It may, therefore, be characterized by two major factors[6] such as: (i) "cost of compliance" which may be evaluated in respect of the amount of cost or price, whether material, physical, or psychological, incurred by the 'influencer' in exploiting the resources for securing the compliance of the 'influencee', and (ii) "probability of compliance" which may be evaluated in respect of spontaneity or reluctance of the 'influencee' in rendering compliance to the intention of the 'influencer'. Accordingly, the cost of compliance may be high or low, and the probability of compliance may also be high or low; and hence, there may be discerned two different patterns of influence-relationship such as: (i) 'Influence' involving 'low cost' of compliance and 'high probability' of compliance which may be termed as "spontaneous-influence" because the 'influencee' spontaneously renders compliance to the intention of the 'influencer' believing in the latter's goodwill and benevolence, and therefore, the 'influencer' is able to bring about desired changes in the behaviour of the 'influencee' easily, and the cost of securing compliance becomes minimal for him; and (ii) 'Influence' involving 'high cost' of compliance and 'low probability' of compliance which may be termed as 'coercive-influence' because the 'influencee' feels coerced psychologically, physically, or materially, and hence, renders compliance, with great reluctance, and the 'influencer', with great difficulty, is able to bring desired changes in the behaviour of the 'influencee' on countering stiff resistance, and he incurs a high cost for securing such compliance. As regard these two types, "spontaneous-influence" may be considered as "influence proper"; whereas "coercive-influence" may be termed as "Power"[7].

3.2 Power

'Power', like influence, is also an inter-personal relationship in which one actor brings about desired changes in the behaviour of another actor or actors but, unlike influence, the former secures compliance of the latter on performing the act of coercion, not the act of inducement or persuasion. On this most discerning attribute, Harold D. Lasswell and Abraham Kaplan emphatically point out: "Power is a special case of the exercise of influence; it is the process of affecting the policies of others with the help of (actual or threatened) severe deprivations for non-conformity with the policies intended"[8]. Similarly, Robert A. Dahl also opines: "Power.......... is a special case of influence involving severe losses for non-compliance."[9]

These notions precisely focus on "Power" as a kind of influence but with a distinctiveness of its own. No doubt, both these phenomena are concerned with bringing about desired changes in others' behaviour but the methods or means of bringing about such changes are different. In case of 'influence-relationship', desired change in the behaviour of the 'influencee' is brought about on inducing or persuading him; whereas in case of 'power-relationship', desired change in the behaviour of the "power-addressee" is brought about by the "power-holder" on exploiting his resources in such a way that the former feels coerced, and renders compliance. Moreover, 'influence-relationship' involving 'low-cost' of compliance, and 'high-probability' of compliance enables the 'influencer' to secure the compliance of the 'influencee' easily, and also it creates a congenial situation in which the latter is induced to render compliance spontaneously. But, 'power-relationship', as it involves 'low probability' of compliance and 'high-cost' of compliance, creates a situation in which the 'power-holder' secures the compliance of the 'power-addressee' with great difficulty, and also the latter renders compliance with great reluctance. Hence, in 'power-relationship', the "power-holder" uses his resources in such a way as to cause actual or threatened loss or deprivation to the "power-addressee" in respect of valued things or objects such as honour, reward, wealth, physical person, or other things that the latter considers valuable. It is actual loss or fear of deprivation for non-compliance that coerces or compels the 'power-addressee' to change his behaviour in complying with the intention and direction of the 'power-holder'. For instance, the 'vehicle-drivers' obey traffic rules and the directions of the 'traffic-police' because of fear of punishment involving loss or deprivation for non-compliance, and hence, there ensues a 'power-relationship' between the 'traffic-police' and the 'vehicle-drivers'. Thus, 'power-relationship' is a relationship between the "power-holder" and the "power-addressee", and is essentially characterized by the attribute of 'coercion' as it is the threat of sanctions issued by the 'power-holder' against the 'power-addressee' that compels the latter to comply with the intentions and directions of the former. Therefore, "Power" may be defined as the superior ability or capability of an actor to bring about desired changes in the behaviour of other actor or actors by the use or threat of use of sanctions.

3.2.1 Locating the Power-Holder

In socio-political situations, the 'power-holder' may be located in various ways on employing various methods. However, there may be discerned, as Robert A. Dahl opines, four major methods[10] of locating the 'power-holder' in relation to the 'power-addressee' in the socio-political process. According to him, the first method is the institutional method which is based on the assumption that power tends to be institutionalized, and that it inter-plays within the legal framework of an office or institution. As power is derived from the official position, the amount of power of an officer tends to be correlated with his position or status in the official hierarchy. Therefore, the higher the official position of the officer, the greater may be amount of his power in relation to his subordinates. Accordingly, the rank or position of the 'power-holder' in relation to the 'power-addressee' may be enquired and ascertained in the official or institutional framework. However, the greatest shortcoming of this method is rooted in its formalistic approach because the officer, even if he hold an official position, may not exercise power in reality, and he may be remote-controlled by some other actor who remains outside the office or institution. For instance, in the institutional arrangement of the Government of India, the Prime Minister may be presumed to be the highest power-holder but, in reality, he may be remote-controlled by the President of the Ruling Party or by the Business-tycoons in the discharge of his functions. Hence, this method of locating the 'power-holder' or the greatest powerful person with reference to the official position that he holds in an institution may be erroneous and misleading in reality.

The second method of locating the 'power-holder' focuses and relies upon the opinion of well-placed observers who watch and observe the inter-play of power in and around a formal institution in reality, and on the basis of their opinions, the 'power-holder' may be located. But, the disadvantage of this method is our exclusive dependence on the subjective observations and opinions of the observers who may be biased or prejudiced. Hence, this method also may not be helpful to us to locate the 'power-holder' in reality.

The third method requires that the researcher or the analyst would observe the frequency of participatory activities of the actors in the socio-political decision-making process, and its presumption is that he who most often participates, and is most involved in the decision-making process is the most powerful actor. However, locating the powerful merely on the basis of frequency of participation in the decision-making process of an institution may be fallacious. For instance, the frequency of participation of the Prime Minister of India and his personal secretary in the decision-making process of the Government of India may be equal, but it is erroneous to conclude that the personal secretary is as powerful as the Prime Minister of India. Hence this method is also found to be defective in locating the 'power-holder' or the powerful. On being aware of the shortcomings of the above methods, Dahl proposes the fourth method which requires objective measurement or quantification of the amount of power of the actors involved in the decision-making process of socio-political institutions. It is based on the assumption that the greater the amount of power of an actor, the higher may be his relative status or rank as a 'power-holder', and accordingly the most powerful actor may be located on the basis of possession of the greatest amount of power.

3.2.2 Measurement of Power

The amount of power of an actor in relation to other actors may be empirically measured or quantified, according to Robert A. Dahl[11] and also Harold D. Lasswell[12], with reference to five major factors or variables such as: (i) Base of Power, (ii) Means of Power, (iii) Weight of Power, (iv) Scope of Power, and (v) Domain of Power. The first variable is the "base" of power that refers to the vital resources such as wealth, social status, knowledge and expertise, official and constitutional position, physical strength, military prowess, and charisma etc. from which power or coercive ability may be derived. These resources are to be accurately and precisely measured. The second variable is the "means" of power that refers to the method or technique and skill which may be employed by the actor in order to exploit the resources at his disposal for causing actual or threatened loss or deprivation to others, and thereby, to coerce them to render compliance to his intentions and directions. In power-relationship, the 'power-holder', no doubt, employs coercive means or methods, but while exploiting the resources for coercing the power-addressee to render compliance, he is required to incur the cost, either psychological or physical or material, for securing such compliance. This cost which is borne or incurred by an actor for securing compliance of others would be precisely measured and quantified.

The third variable is the "weight" of power that refers to the extent to which the 'power-addressee' renders compliance to the intention and direction of the 'power-holder'. It requires, as Dahl[13] suggests, precise measurement of the extent of compliance rendered by the 'power-addressee' when power is exercised by the 'power-holder', and also the probable extent of compliance to be rendered by the 'power-addressee' in a hypothetical situation of non-prevalence of power-relationship between the concerned actors. The difference as to the extent of compliance in these two situations may reveal the weight of power of the 'power-holder' on the 'power-addressee'. This formulation may be illustrated in the context of power-relationship between two symbolic actors such as 'A' and 'B' where:

A is the 'power-holder',
B is the 'power-addressee',
P is the power-act of 'A' against 'B',
Q is the absence of power-act of 'A'
X is the extent of compliance of 'B' to 'A's intention or direction when 'A' undertakes 'P' (power-act)
Y is the extent of compliance of 'B' to 'A's intention when 'A' does 'Q' (absence of power-act)
M is the weight of power of 'A' on 'B'

In this power-relationship between 'A' and 'B',

$$M = BX/AP - BX/AQ = X - Y$$

And, "M" may be greatest if the value of "X" will be 1 or more, and the value of "Y" will be zero.
But, if "X" = "Y", it may be inferred that "A" does not have any weight of power against "B", and there does not prevail any 'power-relationship' between them.

For the purpose of conceptual clarity of the variable of 'weight of power', let us analyse an empirical instance of power-relationship between the 'traffic-police' and the 'vehicle drivers'. When the 'traffic-police' stands at the traffic-post, and issues directions for vehicle movement, the 'vehicle-drivers' obey all traffic rules for fear of punishment or penalty, and hence, the extent of compliance of the 'power-addressees' to the 'power-holder' is 100 per cent. However, when the traffic-police remains absent at the traffic post, let us say hypothetically, the 'vehicle-drivers' do not obey traffic-rules. In this example, it may be inferred that the weight of power of the 'traffic-police' (the power-holder) is tremendous as the difference between the extent of compliance secured (100%) in the behaviour of the 'vehicle-drivers' in a situation of exercise power by the 'traffic-police', and the extent of compliance secured (nil) in the behaviour of the 'vehicle-drivers' in a situation of non-exercise of power is 100 per cent. On the contrary, for instance, if the vehicle drivers are found to obey all traffic-rules irrespective of the fact as to whether the 'traffic-police' stands at the traffic post or remains absent, it may be inferred that the 'traffic-police' does not have any weight of power on the 'vehicle-drivers' because the latter spontaneously obey traffic-rules without feeling coerced by the sanctions or punishment to be inflicted by the 'traffic-police'. In this case, since compliance is rendered voluntarily, not owing to actual loss or prospective deprivation or a feeling of coercion, there does not prevail a relationship of power between the 'traffic-police' and the 'vehicle-drivers'. Thus, the weight of power of the 'power-holder' may be precisely measured on finding out the difference between the extent of compliance of the 'power-addressee' in a situation of exercise of power, and the probable extent of his compliance in an hypothetical situation of non-exercise of power.

The fourth variable of measurement of power is "scope" of power that refers to the number of issues or items on which power is successfully exercised, and desired changes are brought about in the behaviour of the 'power-addressee'. The fifth variable is "domain" of power that connotes the number of actors on whom power is successfully exercised, and desired changes are brought about in their behaviour.

All these variables, of course, are to be taken into consideration and used conjointly as referral points or factors in measuring the amount of power of an actor in relation to other actors who are involved in the decision-making process of socio-political institutions. On the whole, possession of more resources in respect of both quantity and quality; greater ability (intellectual, physical or material) to bear the cost of securing compliance despite resistance and reluctance of the power-addressee; greater weight of power; greater scope of power; and greater domain of power may vest greater amount of power in an actor, and may make him relatively more powerful as against other actors.

Thus, the analysis of power-relationship may enable us to locate the most powerful and also the other power-holders, and to comprehend the complexities of inter-personal relationships in socio-political situations and arenas. It may also provide us the essential key for appreciating the dynamics of the Political System. However, as the Political System is exclusively concerned with the enactment and effective implementation of authoritative decisions for the people of the Society as a whole, if necessary, by the use or threat of use of sanctions, its power is required to be legitimized. When the power of the Political System is clothed with legitimacy, the institution of "Authority" emerges, and becomes functional.

3.3 Authority

The term "Authority" connotes the legitimate power and influence exercised by the Government of the Political System to secure the compliance and obedience of its people to its decisions, and policies. As Robert A. Dahl points out: "......legitimate power or influence is generally called authority."[14] Its emergence and institutionalization enables the Government to make authoritative decisions for the Society as a whole, and to implement these effectively and smoothly. The Government, no doubt, makes decisions on all societal issues, but these can be effectively implemented, if necessary, on employing physical force through the police and the armed forces. Governmental decisions, therefore, need be backed by sanctions, because the use or threat of use of sanctions entailing actual or prospective loss for non-compliance tends to coerce people, both psychologically and physically, to abide by governmental decisions and orders. However, force or coercion does not constitute a durable basis of political obligation because "will", not force, is the basis of the State, and hence, use of sanctions exclusively for a prolonged period for securing people's compliance and obedience to governmental decisions and orders may create resentment and alienation in the people, and may ultimately result in their disobedience, and socio-political instability. Therefore, the durable and stable basis of political obligation seems to be people's spontaneous and voluntary obedience born out of legitimacy towards the Political System and its Government. Legitimacy, according to Robert A. Dahl, is the belief of the people that "the structure, procedures, acts, decisions, policies, officials, or leaders of the government possess the quality of rightness, propriety, or moral goodness,...the right, in short, to make binding rules."[15] It is, thus, a system of belief that recognizes the legality, justness and goodness of the Government, and motivates the people to render spontaneous obedience to its decisions. Therefore, legitimacy maximizes the probability and prospect of people's compliance to governmental decisions, minimizes the cost incurred by the Government to secure people's compliance to its decisions, and creates a durable, reliable, and stable basis of political obligation and obedience. Hence, when the power of the Government is legitimized by the people, the Government becomes the 'Authority' of the Political System which, as a consequence, tends to function with great stability and viability.

3.3.1 Types of Authority

As 'Authority' emerges when legitimacy is accorded, its nature and distinguishing attributes seem to be determined by the nature and type of legitimacy. Hence, the source of "Authority" being legitimacy, there may be discerned various types of 'Authority' corresponding to different types of legitimacy. However, a typology of 'Authority' as formulated by Max Weber, an authoritative scholar on this concept, may be adopted for understanding it amply in real-world situations. According to Max Weber, there may be discerned three major types of legitimacy or belief-systems such as: (i) the ration-legal belief system, (ii) the traditional belief-system, and (iii) the charismatic belief-system that constitute the sources for legitimizing the Government, and for generating three corresponding types of "Authority" such as: (i) the Rational-legal Authority, (ii) the Traditional Authority, and (iii) the Charismatic Authority.[16]

The "Ration-legal Authority" emerges from the rational-legal type of legitimacy characterized by the belief of the people in the legality of formal laws and rules.[17] People strongly believe in this formal legal code that specifies the rights and duties of the Government, and spells out the ways that shall be followed by it for exercising its legitimate power. This type of belief-system or legitimacy generates and institutionalizes a type of authority which is termed as "Rational-legal Authority". It emerges in a Society whose people belief in the sanctity of the Constitution as the fundamental law of the land, and also as the source of power of the Government. Hence, the Government derives legitimate power to rule, and to make decisions for the people from deliberately framed fundamental laws or legal provisions as enshrined in the Constitution. As such, the Government, on being clothed with legitimacy, becomes the "Rational-legal Authority", and is required to exercise its power in conformity with the constitutional provisions, and to limit itself to the functional jurisdiction specified by the Constitution. If the incumbents of the Government violate or transgress the provisions of the Constitution, they lose legitimate power or authority to rule and govern over the people. Thus, in case of "Rational-legal Authority", political obligation of the people emanates from their belief in the sanctity of Constitution; and obedience, in reality, is rendered, not to the incumbents of Authority, but to the impersonal constitutional order. In the present-day world, this type of 'Authority' characterizes the Government of all those Political Societies which uphold the supremacy of their respective Constitutions, and are ruled accordingly, as for instance the governmental Authority of U.S.A., U.K., France, Russia, China, India etc.

As different from the "Rational-legal Authority", the "Traditional Authority" emerges from the belief of the people of a Society in the sanctity of immemorial traditions and customs.[18] The incumbent of "Traditional Authority" derives the right to exercise legitimate power from the long-established and practiced customs and traditions which are held in high reverence by the people of the concerned traditional society. As regard this type, the authority of a tribal ruler or chieftain of a primitive or tribal society such as the Society of the Eskimos in the Antartica region, the Society of the Bergdama, and the kingdom of Ouagadougou in Africa may be cited as instances[19]. Thus, in case of the "Traditional Authority", political obligation of the people emanates from their staunch belief in the sanctity of customs and traditions; and people render obedience, in reality, not to the incumbent of 'Authority' but to the 'traditional order'. As Max Weber points out: "Here the obligation of obedience is not based on impersonal order, but is a matter of personal loyalty within the area of accustomed obligation."[20]

On the contrary, the "Charismatic Authority" emerges from the unflinching belief of the people in the charisma of an individual. The source that legitimizes the use of power and influence by the incumbent of this type of 'Authority' is his own charisma which is defined by Weber as "a certain quality of an individual personality by virtue of which he is set apart by ordinary men, and treated as endowed with super-natural, super-human, or at least specifically exceptional power and qualities."[21] Charisma is, thus, an individual's personal attribute that enchants the people, motivates them to render obedience to him, and simultaneously enables the incumbent to exercise legitimate power and influence over them. As regard this type, the authority of Adolf Hitler's Government in Germany from 1934 to 1945, and that of Benito Mussolini's Government in Italy from 1925 to 1943 may be cited as instances. Thus, in case of "Charismatic Authority", political obligation emanates from the belief of the people in the charisma of the incumbent; and obedience is rendered directly to him as charisma is inherent in his personality.

These three types of "Authority", however, differ widely from one another in respect of the scope of power and influence as exercised by the incumbents. In case of the "Charismatic Authority", the scope of power and influence of the incumbent is absolute and unlimited because the source as well as the incumbent of "Authority" are one and the same. As charisma which is the source of this type of "Authority" inheres in, and inseparable from the personality of the incumbent, and as it legitimizes the exercise power and influence by him, there is, indeed, no limit to the scope of his power and influence except the limit that he would decide for himself. But, in case of the "Traditional Authority", and the "Rational-legal Authority", the source of authority and the incumbent are not same but different. As regard the "Traditional Authority", legitimacy for exercising power and influence is derived from long-established and practiced customs and traditions of the people, and hence, the scope of power and influence of the incumbent are limited by these customs and traditions. Of course, as the customs and traditions are not codified but are orally transmitted, there seems to be some scope for arbitrary exercise of power and influence by the incumbent of the 'Traditional-Authority'. On the contrary, in case of the "Rational-legal Authority", legitimacy is derived from deliberately framed and codified laws and rules, and hence, there seems to be no scope for arbitrary exercise of power and influence by the incumbent. Thus, the "Rational-legal Authority" does not have any scope for arbitrary exercise of power and influence; whereas there may be available some scope for arbitrary exercise of power and influence by the incumbent of the "Traditional Authority", and there is unlimited scope for the arbitrary exercise of power and influence by the incumbent of the "Charismatic Authority".

Moreover, these three types of Authority also differ from one another as regard the prospect of stability and durability. In case of the "Rational-legal Authority", and the "Traditional Authority", the source of authority and the incumbent being different and separate, criticism of and dissatisfaction of the people with the incumbents may not mean criticism and disfavour with the source of 'Authority'. If people are dissatisfied against the incumbent of 'Authority', and do not like his policies and roles, the incumbent may be removed or replaced, but the source of 'Authority' would remain intact without any change. For instance, if the people of India become dissatisfied with the role of the Prime Minster, it does not mean dissatisfaction with the Constitution of India. Similarly, if people of a tribal polity become dissatisfied with the role of the tribal chieftain, it does not mean dissatisfaction with the tribal customs and traditions. Thus, in case of both the "Traditional Authority", and the "Rational Legal Authority", disaffection with the incumbents does not mean dissatisfaction with the source of 'Authority', and hence, the disliked incumbent may be removed or replaced without the "source" of authority being changed. Consequently, these two types of Authority would remain stable and durable as long as the source of Authority is not disliked by the people. However, in case of the "Charismatic Authority", the incumbent and the source of 'Authority' being one and the same, criticism of and dissatisfaction with the incumbent would inevitably imply disaffection with the source of 'Authority'. Hence, the "Charismatic Authority" may become unstable and short-lived. Because of this inherent weakness, the "Charismatic Authority" tends to be institutionalized on transforming itself structurally either as the 'Rational Legal Authority' or the 'Traditional Authority'. This process of transformation of the "Charismatic Authority" is termed by Weber as "routinization of charisma'[22]. In this context Weber points out: "In the process of routinization, the charismatic element does not necessarily disappear. It becomes, rather, dissociated from the person of the individual leader and embodied in an objective institutional structure so that the new holders of authority exercise it, at second remove as it were, by virtue of an institutionally legitimized status or office."[23]

3.3.2 Inference

The three types of "Authority" as discerned and classified by Max Weber are, however, ideal or pure types because the 'Authority', in no actual Political Society, is found to contain the attribute of one type exclusively without revealing the attributes of other types. In reality, the 'Authority' of a Political Society is found to contain the attributes or elements of all the three types conjointly. For instance, the 'Authority' of the Government of India is predominantly the rational-legal type, yet it also contains traditional as well as charismatic elements. No doubt, the Government of India and its incumbents derive and exercise legitimate power and influence from the Constitution of India, yet traditional elements are implicit in the behaviour of the Indian people in rendering obedience to the Government's decisions. The present day citizens of India believe in, and accept the legality of the Constitution of India and render habitual obedience to it even if they have not enacted it directly. In that sense, the 'Authority' of the Government of India contains traditional elements. Moreover, it also contains a charismatic element, at least in the negative sense that persistent failure, for prolonged time, of the policies of the Council of Ministers would, most likely, generate disaffection and alienation towards the Government as well as the Constitution; and people may make demands for changing the constitutional order. Thus, the 'Authority' of the Government of India, in reality, contains elements of Weber's three types of 'Authority'.

Therefore, the "Authority" of a Political Society, indeed, contains the charismatic, the traditional and the rational-legal elements conjointly. However, the pattern of combination of these three elements and the predominance of one element as against other elements seem to be crucially determined by the level of modernity of the concerned Political Society. In case of a modern Political Society, its "Authority" may be the rational-legal type predominantly; whereas the traditional authority may be the predominant type in case of the traditional and the transitional Political Society. Therefore, the higher the level of modernity of the Political Society, the greater may be the prospect of emergence of the "Rational-legal Authority" and the predominance of the rational-legal element as against the traditional and charismatic elements in it.

REFERENCES

1. David Easton: *The Political System: An Inquiry into the state of Political Science.* (Calcutta: Scientific Book Company, Indian Edition, 1971) p. 129. Originally published by Alfred A. Knoff Co., New York in 1953.
2. Robert A. Dahl: 'The Concept of Power,' *Behavioural Science*, July 1957, Re-printed in John H. Kessel, G.F. Cole, and R.G. Seddig (eds), *Micro-Politics* (New York: Holt Rinehart & Winston Inc, 1970) p. 568.
3. Robert A. Dahl: *Modern Political Analysis.* (New Delhi: Prentice-Hall of India, 1972, Indian Reprint) p. 32. Originally published in U.S.A. by Prentice-Hall, Englewood Cliffs, N.J. in 1970.
4. *Ibid.*, p. 17.
5. Harold D. Lasswell and Abraham Kaplanm, *Power and Society.* (New Haven: Yale University Press, 1961) p. 71.
6. Robert A. Dahl: *Modern Political Analysis. Op. cit.*, pp. 21-22.
7. *Ibid.*, pp. 32-33.
8. Harold D. Lasswell and Abraham Kaplan: *Power and Society. Op. cit.*, p. 76.
9. Robert A. Dahl: *Modern Political Analysis. Op. cit.* p. 32.
10. *Ibid.*, pp. 26-28.
11. *Ibid.*, pp. 190-226.
    Also Robert A. Dahl: "The Concept of Power". *Op. cit.* pp. 567-579.
12. Harold. D. Lasswell and Abraham Kaplan: *Power and Society. Op. cit.* p. 73.
13. Robert A. Dahl: 'The Concept of Power'. *Op. cit.* pp. 571-572.
14. Robert A. Dahl: *Modern Political Analysis. Op. cit.* p. 33.
15. *Ibid.*, p. 41.
16. Max Weber: The Theory of Social and Economic Organization. (ed.) Talcott Parsons. (New York: The Free Press, 1947) p. 328.
17. *Ibid.*, p. 328.
18. *Ibid.*, p. 328.
19. Gabriel A. Almond and G.B. Powell, Jr: *Comparative Politics: A Developmental Approach.* (New Delhi: Amerind Publishing Co., Indian Reprint, 1975) pp. 218 and 223. Originally published by Little, Brown & Co., Boston, U.S.A. in 1966.
20. Max Weber: *The Theory of Social and Economic Organization. Op. cit.* p. 328.
21. *Ibid.*, p. 358.
22. *Ibid.*, p. 67.
23. *Ibid.*, p. 67.

4

Political Power-Structure

4.1 The Concept

In every Political Society, "Authority" tends to be characterized by a distinct pattern of inter-play of legitimate power in the context of making of decisions on societal issues. It is the pattern of inter-play of legitimate power that forms the "Political Power-Structure" of the Society, and gives it a distinct shape. However, since the exercise of power and influence necessitates possession of vital resources, motivation, and skill; and since these three prerequisites are possessed and monopolized by a few individuals because of natural scarcity of resources and natural inequality of talent, the power-holders and the influential, in every Society, constitute a numerical minority of its population. These few power-holders and influential become the decision-makers in the Society because they control the behaviour of the mass of people, and secure their compliance on performing the acts of inducement and coercion; and hence, they may be termed as 'the Elites' of the Society. The interrelationship among these "Elites" as well as their relationship with the mass of people in the context of inter-play of legitimate power in making and implementing societal decisions and policies constitute the "Political Power-Structure". The "Elites" are the incumbents of this "Political Power-Structure" and they operate it. Thus, 'elite-rule' is inevitable in every Society. It is manifestly evident in case of the 'Authoritarian Political Societies'; whereas it is latently noticed in case of the 'Democratic Political Societies' where the elites, in reality, control and manipulate skilfully the entire electoral process, from the time of nomination of the candidates to their electoral victory. Moreover, in the 'Democratic Political Societies', the elites play dominant and determining roles, directly or indirectly, in context of formation of Government and enactment of public policies as well. Therefore, though Democracy is believed to champion the principle of 'people's-rule', there prevails, in reality, "elite-rule"; and as a consequence, the democratic principles and norms seem to be untrue and irrelevant in practice. Thus, in every Political Society, there is found 'elite-rule' as its 'power-structure', in reality, is composed and operated by the elites. However, the 'political power-structure' may be composed of and be operated by a single, cohesive group of elites or a multiplicity of elite-groups. Accordingly, there may be discerned two major models[1] of "Political Power-Structure" such as (i) the Monolithic-Pyramidal Model and (ii) the Pluralistic-Polyarchal Model.

4.2 The Monolithic-Pyramidal Model

The basic assumption of the "Monolithic-Pyramidal Model" is that the "Political Power-Structure" of the Society is just like a single pyramid where legitimate power for making societal decisions is concentrated in a single centre or only one group composed of the elites. The elites who are the power-holders and the influential in the Society constitute a numerical minority of its population, and presenting themselves as a single, cohesive group of decision-makers, they play key and determining roles in making decisions on all societal issues. The decisions made by them are of such wide scope, affecting the Society as a whole, that these are usually regarded as political decisions[2] even if they are not politicians in the usual and formal sense of the members of the government or the legislature. The elites not only make societal decisions but they also implement these decisions effectively on securing the obedience of the people on employing both coercive and persuasive measures.

Thus, the elites who constitute a numerical minority of the society's population rule and dominate over the majority of its people. At the same time, the "ruling elite-group" cannot be controlled by the majority or the mass of population because of unity among the elites. As James Meisel[3] points out, the "ruling elite-group" is characterized by 3 Cs' such as: (i) Consciousness, (ii) Cohesion, and (iii) Conspiracy. The elites are conscious of their superior status in the Society as its decision-makers; and they have a common will to action to maintain and perpetuate their superior status. They undertake endeavours for maintaining their dominance on increasing the amount of power by way of acquiring more and more vital resources and exploiting these skilfully in order to obtain obedience of the people to their decisions. They also tend to perpetuate 'elite-rule' in Society on permitting limited entry into their group for a few selected individuals who conform to the parameters of their higher status in terms of socio-economic and cultural background, and ideological commitments.

Thus, the "Monolithic-Pyramidal Model" lays down and asserts the following fundamental propositions: (i) the Society's 'political power-structure' is composed of, and operated by the elites who are a few persons in number, and who always present themselves as a single and cohesive group of decision-makers on all societal issues; (ii) it is uni-centic in structure because the legitimate power of making authoritative or binding decisions for the Society remains vested in the single "ruling elite-group", and hence, there is only one centre of power in the Society; (iii) it is also pyramidal in structure because the elite-group consists of two strata of elites such as the stratum of the core decision-makers and the stratum of the potential decision-makers, and between these two strata, the core-stratum consists of an extremely small number of persons but the potential-stratum exceedingly out-numbers the former; (iv) the "ruling elite-group", even though it is composed of a minority of individuals, cannot be controlled by the mass or the large majority of the population of the Society, rather the people are controlled by the 'ruling elite-group'; (v) the power of the elite-group is cumulative in the sense that it is ever-increasing as power is used to accumulate and harness new and additional resources; and (vi) the "ruling elite-group" tends to perpetuate itself on providing, if necessary, the entry of an extremely limited number of individuals from the mass of people into its circle, and also imbuing the new entrants with elite-values. However, within the general thesis of the "Monolithic-Pyramidal Model" that portrays Society's "Political Power-Structure" as essentially uni-centric and pyramidal, and asserts the rule by a single cohesive group of elites, important differences may be noted among the classical elite-theorists as to the key to elite-domination and control in Society. Keeping in view these scholarly differences on this central concern of the "Monolithic-Pyramidal Model" or the "Ruling Elite Model" of Society's "Political Power-Structure", there may be discerned four major perspectives or approaches[4] such as: (i) Organizational Approach, (ii) Psychological Approach, (iii) Economic Approach, and (iv) Institutional Approach.

4.2.1 Organizational Approach

This approach for understanding and explaining the political power-structure of the Society is advocated by Gaetano Mosca and Roberto Michels, though they widely differ as to the key to elite-domination and control.

Mosca, in his book '*The Ruling Class*'[5], asserts: "In all societies.... two classes of people appear—a class that rules and a class that is ruled. The first class, always the less numerous, performs all political functions, monopolizes power and enjoys the advantages that power brings, whereas the second, the more numerous class, is directed and controlled by the first, in a manner that is now more or less legal, now more or less arbitrary and violent, and supplies the first, in appearance at least, with material means of subsistence and with the instrumentalities that are essential to the vitality of the political Organism".[6] Thus, Mosca divides the people of the Society into two classes such as the "ruling-class" and the "ruled-class", the former being composed of a numerical minority of the population, and the latter being constituted of the rest of the population who are in a larger numerical majority as compared to the former.

According to Mosca, the "ruling-class" is composed of the elites, and it presents itself always as a highly organized cohesive group. Its unity and cohesion, and its ability to become solidly organized are derived from the smallness of its size. Its internal channels of communication and information are much simpler, and its members can be contacted more speedily as compared to the "ruled-class" which is composed of a large majority of the population. Hence, the elite-group is capable of presenting itself always with complete solidarity of organization, and unity of purpose and action; whereas the "ruled-class" stands thoroughly disorganized, and presents itself always merely as a large aggregation of individuals without a common purpose, and without any quick and effective system of communication of information, and co-ordination of action. The relationship between the ruling-class and the ruled-class, and the sources of strength of the former, and weakness of the latter are emphatically presented by Mosca when he points out: "The power of any minority is irresistible as against each single individual in the majority who stands alone before the totality of the organized minority".[7] Thus, Mosca traces the key to elite-domination and control in Society to the superior organizational ability of the elites themselves. However, he traces the key to the survival and perpetuation of elite-rule to the ruling elite-group's policy and strategy of recruitment of new members into its fold. When there emerges resentment of the people against the policies and decisions of the ruling-class, the latter undertakes coercive or persuasive measures, as deemed necessary, to put down or pacify such resentment and dissatisfaction. Moreover, if necessary, it may change its policies to keep the people satisfied, but it may retain its original composition in respect of membership. However, if these measures are found inadequate to put down people's resentment, it may admit a few representatives of the people into the "ruling-class". For admitting the new members, it lays down terms and conditions which may include standards of wealth, social background, educational attainment, and commitment to the interests and ideology of the ruling elite-group. The new entrants are required to conform to these terms and conditions in order to enable them to enter into the ruling-class. Therefore, the ruling-class is not a closed group of elites, but it provides for limited entry of the representatives of new interests and emerging forces into its circle from time to time. However, as the ruling-class is composed of two strata of elites such as (i) the upper stratum of elites or core decision-makers, and (ii) the lower stratum of elites or potential decision-makers, the new entrants are initially admitted into the lower-stratum of the ruling-class. The entry of the new members into the ruling-class helps to rejuvenate and re-invigorate it as it is brought into contact with the interests and aspirations of the ruled-class. Simultaneously, the new members acquire the spirit and values of the old elites, and become conscious of their newly gained superior status in relation to the rest of the population. Therefore, due to gradual infiltration into the ruling-class by a few chosen members of the ruled-class, there takes place a fusion of the old and the new elements in the ruling-class; and with renewed vigour and zeal, the ruling-class is enabled to maintain and perpetuate its rule and dominance over the people through time. Thus, Mosca traces the key to elite-rule to the superb organizational ability of the elite-group in keeping itself as a cohesive ruling-class, and also he traces the key to its survival and perpetuation to its ultimate strategy of admitting into its fold a few ablest and selected persons of the ruled-class who represent new interests and emerging forces in Society from time to time.

Quite different from the central theme of Mosca's organizational approach, Robert Michels, in his book "Political Parties", advocates an organizational approach that traces the key to elite-domination and control in Society, not to the organizational cohesiveness of the elite-group, but to the organizational necessity of the Society. According to Michels, for a Society to exist and survive through time, it must be organized in the sense that its goals and objectives must be determined; and policies, rules, and regulations must be enacted and implemented effectively so as to establish a situation of social order and peace. For the purpose of successful policy-formulation and implementation, human talent, intellect, and intelligence become necessary; and these intellectual capabilities are naturally found inherent in a few individuals, not in the mass of people who are amateur individuals and laymen. Therefore, leadership for making and implementing public-polices for attainment of societal goals is naturally vested in a few intellectually superior and talented individuals who may be termed as the "Elites". Of course, though the emergence of the elites as the decision-makers of the Society is caused by the technical indispensability of leadership in facilitating the survival of the societal organization, the elites, who are clever and intelligent individuals, take the advantage of the peculiar psychology of the mass-mind in perpetuating their domination and rule over the people. In this context, Michels believes that most of the people are apathetic, indolent, ignorant, and slavish, and they are too glad to have others assume responsibility for them. This peculiar mass-psychology characterized by the need for guidance is taken advantage of by the elites who assume leadership roles, and undertake endeavours, with great unity of purpose, to maintain and perpetuate themselves as decision-makers of the Society.

The elite-rule, according to Michels, establishes 'Oligarchy' in Society, and it is so stable that, normally, there would never be any absolute change or displacement of the ruling-class by the ruled-class. However, Michels admits, a few new members, from the ruled-class, who represent new interests and emerging social forces, may be admitted into the ruling-class as and when necessary, but it simply brings about an amalgamation of new elements with the old ones in the sense that the character of the "ruling elite-group" never undergoes any vital change. On the contrary, the new members who are admitted into the ruling-class gradually assume the character of its members. Of course, Michels does not deny that the mass or members of the ruled-class do not revolt from time to time but he is of the opinion that, even though revolts are organized by the ruled-class against the ruling-class, these are always suppressed, and that rarely, a revolution may become successful. However, he emphatically points outs that the success of a revolution does not mean end of the elite-rule, because the mass of people cannot revolt without leaders, and that these leaders having acquired power in the name of the people quickly transform themselves into a relatively closed class of elites. Elite-rule is, thus, inevitable and universal for every Society. Hence, Michels issues his celebrated formulation: "who says organization, says oligarchy."[9]

4.2.2 Psychological Approach

This approach for understanding and explaining the "Monolithic-Pyramidal Model" of "Political Power-structure" of the Society is propounded by Vilfredo Pareto in his work "Mind and Society".[10] According to Pareto, those individuals who hold top and leading positions in different branches of human activity in the Society may be termed as 'Elites'. However, the elites of the Society may be classified into two categories such as "Governing Elites" and "Non-governing Elites". Those elites who are involved with the decision-making and governing process of the Society are termed by Pareto as the "Governing Elites"; and he analyses their roles, and their relationship with the rest of the population (the mass), especially, in view of their psychological make-up for understanding the nature and dynamics of the "political power-structure".

Pareto undertakes his analysis with the basic assumption that psychology of the individual determines his activities and behaviour. According to him, human psychology is characterized by distinct instincts or tendencies, what he terms as 'Residues', that remain permanent, and constant in him, and that tend to determine all his activities and behaviour. These "Residues" are classified by him into two broad categories such as: (i) Class I Residues that reflect "the instinct of combination", i.e. the impulse to put together ideas that are formed through imagination, invention, and reflection, and (ii) Class II Residues that reflect "the instinct of persistence of aggregates", i.e. the tendency to consolidate values and positions once these are acquired and established, and to maintain stability and order.

According to Pareto, in the psychology of every individual, there may be found a predominance of either Class I Residues, or Class II Residues. If Class I Residues predominate his psychology, he is most likely to become clever, cunning and intelligent, and to display 'Fox-like qualities' in his thinking and activities; whereas the predominance of Class II Resides in him would, most likely, make him a man of strength and integrity, and a man who is ardently devoted to maintenance of order, discipline, and stability; and thus, there would be manifested "Lion-like qualities" in his thinking and activities. Thus, every individual is either 'a Fox' or 'a Lion' in his psychology and behaviour. However, on observation of the psychology and behaviour of the "governing-elites" and also of the "mass of people", Pareto finds that Class II Residues, i.e. lion-like qualities characterized by tendencies for stability and order, and attachment for customs and traditions are predominant in the psychology of the mass of the population; whereas the "governing-elites" may have a predominance of either Class I Residues, i.e. fox like qualities, or Class II Residues, i.e. lion-like qualities in their psychology. Hence, the 'governing-elites' may be classified into two groups such as: (i) the group of Foxes, i.e. elites with predominance of Class I Residues characterized by fox-like qualities, and (ii) the group of Lions, i.e. elites with predominance of Class II Residues characterized by lion-like qualities. It is the psychological make-up of the elites of the "governing-group" that tends to determine, Pareto believes, the style of governance in a Society at a given period of time.

Pareto is of the opinion that the style of governance by the "Foxes" is significantly different from that by the "Lions", as it manifests and reflects the distinctive quality of the psychology that characterizes each group of governing-elites. The "Foxes" are intelligent, clever, and cunning; and, in governing the people, their ultimate objective is to gain popular support necessary for their continuance as the decision-makers of the Society. Therefore, for keeping the people satisfied they devise ideologies and policies not only to bring about economic and material development of the people but also to solve immediate crises and problems. Though the 'Foxes' are distinguished by their political astuteness, ingenuity and manoeuvering, they are reluctant to use force for maintaining order and discipline in the Society. As different from the 'Foxes', 'the Lions' are, not men of ideas and ingenuity to attract the people, but are tough-minded and ruthless in governing the latter for maintaining societal customs and traditions as well as order and stability. Thus, each of group of the 'governing-elites', i.e. the group of "Foxes" and the group of "Lions", is found to be lacking in a vital quality necessary for stable and durable governance. The group of "Foxes" are reluctant to use force which is necessary for maintaining order in the Society; whereas the group of "Lions" lack in ideas and ingenuity necessary for devising policies for bringing about socio-economic development of the people, and recruiting their support for the government. Therefore, Pareto hypothesizes that the displacement and replacement of one group of "governing-elites" by another group is inevitable. According to him, there takes place a constant alternation between the group of tender-minded "Foxes" and the group of tough-minded "Lions". As the "Foxes" are reluctant to use force for maintaining societal order, they ultimately become ineffective, and their rule degenerates into chaos and political instability. This deficiency of the group of "Foxes" is taken advantage by the group of tough-minded "Lions" who became impatient to restore order and strong government, take the leadership of the people, and violently over-throw the Government of the "Foxes". Thus, the governing-group of "Foxes" is replaced by the group of "Lions". The Government of the "Lions", no doubt, establishes societal order and stability, but it lacks in intellectual ability to devise policies and schemes for socio-economic development of the people. Simultaneously, its toughness to use force for maintaining order and stability generates and fosters dissatisfaction in the people against its rule and governance. Therefore, for reducing people's resentment against its rule and keeping them satisfied by way of enacting schemes of economic development, the governing group of "Lions" feels compelled to remedy its intellectual deficiency on allowing entry of a few "Foxes" into the Government. Once the "Foxes" enter into the Government, they gradually increase their number, and use their political ingenuity to replace the Government of the "Lions" by the Government of the "Foxes" ultimately.

Thus, in Pareto's formulation, the process of replacement of the groups of "Governing-Elites" occurs in two ways: (i) firstly, by a gradual process of infiltration, what Pareto terms as 'Circulation of Elites', when the "Foxes" gradually infiltrate into the governing-group of "Lions", and (ii) secondly, by a violent over-throw when the governing-group of "Foxes" is totally replaced by the "Lions". Though, one group of "governing-elites" is replaced by another group, i.e. the "Foxes" by the "Lions", and *viceversa*, either by way of violent over-throw or gradual infiltration, Pareto is of the opinion that there takes place no vital transformation in the 'political power-structure' of the Society. He asserts that Society is always ruled by a group of "Governing-Elites" which is composed of either "Foxes" or "Lions", though the style of governance changes in accordance with the psychological make-up of the "governing-elites" at a given period of time in the socio-political process of the Society. Thus, "elite-rule" is permanent as people need leaders; and the Society's 'political power-structure' is characterized by the 'monolithic-pyramidal model' because the 'governing-elite group' always works with unity and cohesion; and whether it is composed of the "Foxes" or the "Lions" at given period of time, it perpetually rules over the people, and thus, there is no end to "elite-rule".

4.2.3 Economic Approach

This approach for explaining the "Monolithic-Pyramidal Model" of "Political Power-Structure" of the Society is expounded by James Burnham who, in his book 'The Managerial revolution', identifies the economic factor as the key to elite-domination and rule. According to him, the chief source of power of the elites is decidedly economic, because it is control over the major means of production that gives an individual or a group the dominant position in Society. He observes that the controllers of the major means of production constitute a small numerical minority of the population; and that they enjoy not only economic advantages but also social prestige and political power, and make themselves the decision-makers of the Society because economic power paves for political power. These economic-elites, thus, constitute a close-knit group that plays determining and dominant roles in the process of making of public policies. It is this elite-group that designs the State and its institutions, and enacts laws and public policies so as to maintain and perpetuate the capitalist system of economic control with its concomitant relations of production for the benefit of the capitalist class. However, as Burnham points out, success or failure of the "capitalist-class" in perpetuating itself in power depends upon its ability to monopolize and control the major means of production for long. Since monopoly over the process of production necessitates prevention of others from gaining access to the means of production, the "capitalist-class" may remain as economic-controllers and political decision-makers so long as it is able to prevent new entrants to gain access to the process of production, and to control the techniques or forces of production. But, Burnham believes, it may not be possible for the capitalist-class to retain its monopoly and control over the productive process for long because of the necessity to modernize the techniques of production for increasing the products in terms of both quantity and quality. For modernizing the techniques of production, persons with technical knowledge and expertise are to be recruited and appointed, and with their entry into the productive process, economic control that was originally exercised by the Capitalists would gradually decline. Thus, management and control over the productive process would ultimately be vested in the technocrats and professional managers; whereas the Capitalists would remain merely as financiers of the enterprises, and constitute a leisured class of economic-elites. Therefore, Burnham believes, because of technical indispensability of the technocrats and professional managers for operating the productive process and deciding investment policies, a new class of "Managerial-Elites" would emerge in every modern Society, and it would control and manage not only the productive process but also the political process of the Society. In this context, projecting forward trends that are apparent in modern Societies, Burnham predicts that the Government will increasingly be concerned with executive action rather than legislation, and will be run by bureaucrats who are more akin in out-look and expertise to the industrial managers than to the laymen "politicians" of the capitalist era. As economic power paves for political power, the class of the "Managerial-Elites" would control the "State-apparatus", and there would ensue the process of inter-change of industrial managers and bureaucrats. Thus, the new class of "Managerial-Elites" would consolidate itself, would present a united front, and perpetuate its domination and rule over the people in the Society through time.

4.2.4 Institutional Approach

This approach which is expounded by C. Wright Mills in his book, 'Power Elite'[12] envisions the 'political power-structure' of the Society in the "Monolithic-Pyramidal" perspective but considers the institutional landscape of the Society as the chief source of power of the ruling-group of elites. The basic assumption of this approach is that power tends to be institutionalized. According to Wright Mills, there is inter-play of power in, and around key institutions of the Society, and hence, those individuals who hold top positions or strategic command posts in these key institutions become, in reality, the power-holders, and decision-makers of the Society. They may be termed as 'Power-Elites', and they always present themselves as a conscious and cohesive group of power-wielders in relation to the rest of the population.

C. Wright Mills, in his study of the American Society, locates the "power-elites" in three major or strategic institutions such as the Military, the Big Corporations, and the Political Executive. According to him, the leaders or top individuals who occupy command positions in these three key institutions in U.S.A. constitute the group of "power-elites", and make decisions on all major policy-issues in the American Society. These "power-elites" always stand united, and their cohesiveness results from, 'institutional proximity'[13], among these key institutions as evident from the easy "inter-change of commanding roles at the top of one institutional order with those in another."[14] He cites, as instances, the numerous cases of Chair-persons and Directors of Big Business Corporations who have taken up major posts in the Government of U.S.A., and have subsequently retuned to Business Corporations and Foundations. The ease with which the inter-change of roles takes place amply indicates the high degree of cohesiveness among the elites.

Thus, the core of Wright Mills analysis is that the power to make decisions on societal issues remains vested in the hands of a few individuals who hold command posts in key and strategic institutions in the Society. They constitute a highly conscious and cohesive group of "Power-Elites", and they dominate over and control the people who stand fragmented and subdued, and are even unaware of the role they can play in the total societal-structure. Hence, the "Political Power-Structure" of the Society is decidedly elitist with monolithic attributes.

4.2.5 Approaches: Diversities and Consensus

The approaches to the study and analysis of the "Monolithic-Pyramidal Model" of "Political Power-Structure" of the Society are found to reveal significant diversities among them. The classical elite-theorists such as Gaetano Mosca, Roberto Michels, Vilfredo Pareto, James Burnham, and C. Wright Mills who are the proponents of their respective approaches tend to view the coherence and solidarity of the "ruling elite-group" and its continuing domination over the people of the Society in different perspectives. In this context, the key to elite-domination and control in the Society is traced by Mosca to the organizational ability of the ruling elite-group, by Michels to the organizational necessity of the Society and the indispensability of the elites' leadership, by Pareto to the psychological make-up of both the governing-elites and the mass of people, by Burnham to the control over the chief means of production and the technical indispensability of the managerial-elites, and by C. Wright Mills to the institutional land-scape and the strategic institutions in the Society. However, despite such differences in the visions and views of these classical elite-theorists, all of them are found to have consensual opinions and assertions that legitimate political power in every Society, in reality, is exercised by a single coherent group of "Elites", and that, therefore, the "Political Power-structure" of the Society may be characterized as the "Monolithic-Pyramidal Model".

4.3 The Pluralistic-Polyarchal Model

The chief theorist of the "Pluralistic-Polyarchal Model" of Society's "Political Power-structure" is Robert A. Dahl.[15] Of course, its intellectual roots may be traced to Arthur F. Bentley[16] who, in his book '*The Process of Government*' published in 1908, has laid down the foundation for pluralistic analysis of the Political Society and its power-structure. The views of Bentley have been subsequently upheld by David Truman[17], and reinforced, through empirical investigations, by Robert A. Dahl. The basic assumption of the "Pluralistic-Polyarchal Model" is that Society is a mosaic of groups, and that decisions concerning societal policies are made amidst group-interactions and competitions. Hence, this model, on rejecting the basic assumptions of the "Monolithic-Pyramidal Model" as unrealistic, asserts that Society's "Political Power-structure" is poly-centric in the sense that it is composed of political-elites representing various interest-groups, and that these elites compete with one another for influencing the process of public policy-making in order to protect and promote the cherished interests of their respective groups. The shortcomings of the "Monolithic-Pyramidal Model", what Dahl terms as the "Ruling-elite Model", are succinctly pointed out by him in his work 'A Critique of the Ruling Elite Model'. Dahl is of the opinion that the classical elite-theorists have a mistaken and unrealistic view on the scope of influence and power of the members of the "ruling elite-group" because all vital resources, in reality, are not possessed and monopolized by its members equally but each member may monopolize any one of these vital resources such as wealth, skill and knowledge, social status, military prowess and physical strength, charisma etc., and may exploit it in influencing the decision-making process concerning the issue of his interest. Therefore, though all members of the "ruling elite-group" have potentiality for controlling the decision-making process, each member may not be interested and active equally with every other member in controlling the process of making decisions on all issues and policies. As such, the classical elite-theorists, Dahl opines, confuse the elite's potentiality for control with actual political effectiveness of each, and present a mistaken view of absolute unity and coherence of the ruling-elites in playing their roles in the societal decision-making process.

Moreover, Dahl observes that the various interest-groups, under the leadership of their respective leaders, compete among themselves for becoming successful in realizing their cherished interests on influencing the Government and its decision-making process on employing required devices and strategies of action. Hence, the Society's "Political Power-Structure" tends to be diversified and pluralistic in form and essence, and it is not akin to a single pyramid but to a range of pyramids as leaders and elites representing different interest groups compete and vie with one another to control the public policy-making process to suit with their own objectives, and to reap maximum advantages. Thus, the 'political power-structure' of the Society is not only pluralistic but also poly-archal in the sense that legitimate power for making societal decisions is not vested in a single group of elites but is shared by a number of groups and that these groups function as decision-making centres for making decisions on different societal issues.

However, despite prevalence of socio-political pluralism in the "Democratic Political Society", Dahl observes that its decision-making process is controlled, in reality, by a few elites and leaders who represent various interest-groups and play key roles as and when decisions concerning their respective interests are made. Thus, even though the "political power-structure" is pluralistic and poly-archal, the actual decision-makers are a few elites who constitute a numerical minority *vis-à-vis* the majority of the people of the Society. Therefore, elite-rule or oligarchic-rule is not only evident but inevitable, and this phenomenon emerges because of inequitable distribution of vital resources; monopolization of vital resources by a few persons; and the political in-activism, indifference and apathy of the mass of population of the society. Of course, these elites and leaders do not constitute a single cohesive and conspiratorial group of decision-makers because the 'Democratic Political Society' is essentially a mosaic of groups, and is characterized by competitive politics allowing freedom of political participation to the individuals and groups. These elites and leaders are merely representatives of various groups, and they compete with one another, not on all issues, but on those that pertain to their group-interests, in influencing the process of public policy-making for effective attainment of their respective group-goals. Therefore, even if there is 'elite-rule' in the Democratic Political Society, sovereignty resides in the people, and these elites and leaders who represent the people seek people's mandate and approval to their rule and policies through periodic elections. At the same time, on being indirectly controlled by the people through periodic elections, these political elites or leaders remain diversified and fragmented because they belong to different groups with different interests. Hence, the Democratic Political Society becomes characterized by 'Democratic Elitism', and its political power-structure tends to be "Pluralistic-Polyachal" in form and essence.

4.4 Empirical Tests of the Models

Scholars have undertaken empirical researches, of course, at the community levels, for finding out and ascertaining the validity of both of these models of Society's "Political Power-Structure". For this purpose, a worth-noticing endeavour is that of Floyd Hunter whose findings and observations are contained in his book '*Community Power-structure*'[18] published in 1953. Hunter has undertaken his investigations in the American city of Atlanta in order to find out the essential features of its 'political decision-making structure'. He has employed the reputational approach for listing the elites or the top decision-makers of this city; and he has identified three major areas of activities such as Politics, Business, and Civic Organizations in which he has listed their top and key persons. He has investigated into the pattern of inter-personal relationship among these top leaders, and also their roles in the policy-making process in the city of Atlanta, and has observed that these top elites have constituted not only a conscious, cohesive and conspiratorial group but also have significantly dominated the public life and the policy-making process of this regional city. Hunter, therefore, has concluded that the "Political Power-Structure" of the city of Atlanta is characterized by the essential features of the "Ruling-Elite Model" which is termed as the "Monolithic-Pyramidal Model".

The empirical findings of Floyd Hunter validating the 'Monolithic-Pyramidal Model' of Community's Political Power-structure have been sternly challenged by Robert A. Dahl on the basis of his investigation of the political decision-making process in another American city named "New Haven". Dahl's findings are contained in his famous work 'Who Governs?'[19] and these indicate the validity of the "Pluralistic-Polyarchal Model" as against the "Monolithic-Pyramidal Model" of political power-structure. In undertaking his empirical investigation in the American city of New Haven, Dahl has employed the decision-making approach for identifying its core decision-makers, and has examined their roles in controlling the process of public policy-making. For this purpose, he has selected three major 'issue-areas' such as urban redevelopment, public education system, and political nominations for the post of city-mayor, and has investigated into the participatory roles of persons in the community's decision-making process especially with regard to the frequency of initiation of important policies against opposition, the ability to exercise a veto over policies initiated by others, and the ability to enact the desired policy by exercising influence and power effectively on others. In this investigation, Dahl notices elite-participation in the community's decision-making process. However, the elites who represent different interest groups are found to have neither a common interest nor equal ability to control the process of public policy-making. Rather, their intensity of interest and controlling abilities are found to vary from issue to issue. As such, the elites and leaders of the city of New Haven do not constitute a single cohesive group of decision-makers but are beset with dissensions and diversities. Hence, Dahl on describing the structure of decision-making in New Haven terms it as 'Polyarchy'. This empirical investigation conducted by Dahl vindicates the validity of the "Pluralistic-Polyarchal Model" of the Society's political power-structure.

Empirical investigations for discerning the structure of political power at the community levels have also been undertaken by other scholars, as for instance, Robert Presthus,[20] Robert Agger[21] and his associates, Nelson W. Polsby[22], and Arnold M. Rose[23]. Their findings reveal that communities vary considerably in their respective power-structures, some being pluralistic and other elitist in features and essence. Thus, no conclusive empirical evidence on the universal validity of either the "Monolithic-Pyramidal Model" or the

"Pluralistic-Polyarchal Model" is available till today. However, the fact remains that, political power, in every Society, is unevenly distributed because of inequitable distribution of vital resources among the people; that the elites who are influential and power-holders owing to their monopolization of the vital resources become the decision-makers of the Society; and that they not only constitute its "Political Power-Structure" but also operate it. Of course, formulation of a conclusive universal model to describe the Society's "Political Power-Structure" as to whether it is monolithic or pluralistic, and pyramidal or polyarchal should await further rigorous empirical investigations.

REFERENCES:

1. Geraint Parry, *Political Elites* (London: George Allen & Unwin Ltd., 1969), especially pp. 67, 112, 120-121, 141.
2. *Ibid*., p. 30.
3. James H. Meisel, *The Myth of the Ruling Class: Gaetano Mosca and the Elite*. (Ann Arbor: University of Michigan Press, 1958).
4. Geraint Parry, *Political Elites*, *op. cit.* p. 35.
5. Gaetano Mosca, *The Ruling Class*. (Edited by A. Livingston). (New York: McGraw Hill, 1939).
6. *Ibid*., p. 50.
7. *Ibid*., p. 53.
8. Robert Michels, *Political Parties*. (Glencoe, Illinois: Free Press, 1942), Translated in English in 1915.
9. *Ibid*., p. 418.
10. Vilfredo Pareto, *The Mind and Society*. (New York: Harcourt-Brace, 1935).
11. James Burnham, *The Managerial Revolution*. (New York: Putman, 1942).
12. C. Wright Mills, *The Power Elites*. (New York: Oxford University Press, 1964).
13. *Ibid*., p. 288.
14. *Ibid*., p. 288.
15. Robert A. Dahl:
    (i) 'A Critique of the Ruling Elite Model'. *The American Political Science Review*, Vol. 52 (June 1958), pp. 463-469.
    (ii) *Who Governs*? (New Haven: Yale University Press, 1961.
    (iii) *Polyarchy*. (New Haven: Yale University Press, 1971).

16. Arthur F. Bentley, *The Process of Government* (London: Constable Press, 1908).
17. David Truman, *The Governmental Process*. (New York: Alfred A. Knopf. 1951).
18. Floyd Hunter, *Community Power-Structure*. (New York, Garden City: Anchor Books, 1963).
19. Robert A. Dahl, *Who Governs. Op. cit.*
20. Robert Presthus, *Men at the Top*. (New York: Oxford University Press, 1964).
21. Robert Agger, D. Goldrich and B. Swanson, *The Rulers and the Ruled* (New York: Wiley, 1964).
22. Nelson W. Polsby, *Community Power and Political Theory* (New Haven: Yale University Press, 1963).
23. Arnold M. Rose, *The Power Structure*. (New York: Oxford University Press, 1967).

5

Political Culture

5.1 The Concept

The Political System with its "Authority-Structure" needs legitimacy of the people in order to remain stable and viable. However, accordance or withdrawn of legitimacy seems to be crucially determined by the pattern of people's "Political Culture". If the pattern of political-culture is supportive of the Political System, the latter would, most likely, remain stable and viable, whereas un-supportive or alienated political-culture may cause instability, and even total transformation of the form or "Structure" of the Political System. Hence, the study of the dynamics of the Political System, in the context of "Society-Politics Interactions", inevitably involves discernment of the pattern of political-culture of the people, and analysis of its implications on micro-politics and macro-politics.

'Political-Culture' is a distinct part of 'Societal-Culture'. The term 'Culture', in general, refers to "that complex whole which includes knowledge, belief, art, morals, law, custom and any other capabilities and habits acquired by man as a member of the society."[1] It is a shared way of life of an organized set of individuals, and it shapes the pattern of their social relationships.[2] It encompasses all such knowledge, values and beliefs, both existential and normative, which are socially shared and transmitted from generation to generation.[3] Culture, thus, represents shared psychological orientations of the people of a Society toward societal objects.[4] As individuals or members of a Society interact with one another in recurrent social relationships, they form and develop values, beliefs, sentiments, cognition and attitudes towards these collective endeavours which they share with their fellow-members. This shared societal life facilitates formation of perceptions and orientations in the people toward societal objects such as the various social, economic and political systems and institutions of the Society, and also the varieties of roles that they are required to perform as members of these systems and institutions. Consequently, people of the Society acquire and form, more or less, a distinct pattern of orientations toward societal objects, and it may be termed as the "Societal Culture" or the culture of the people of the Society. Culture is, thus, the web that binds together the people of the Society as it tends to shape individuals' behaviour and roles which, in turn, seems to determine the pattern of societal dynamics.[5]

In the "Societal Culture", there may be noted and discerned "Political Culture" as one of its distinct components. It refers to the pattern of psychological orientations of the people of the Society toward 'Politics' and their 'Political System'. It is defined by Gabriel A. Almond, the founding father of this nomenclature, as "a particular pattern of orientations to political actions"[6]. On elaborating it, he explains: "political culture ….is a set of attitudes—cognitions, value-standards, and feelings—towards the political system, its various roles and role-incumbents. It also includes knowledge of, values affecting, and feelings toward the inputs of demands and claims into the political system, and its authoritative outputs."[7] More precisely, he points out: "when we speak of political culture of a society we refer to the political system as internalized in the cognitions, feelings, and evaluations of its population."[8] Thus, the political-culture, at the level of the individual, characterizes his psychology, which, in turn, Almond[9] asserts, tends to shape and determine his political behaviour and roles. Similarly, at the level of the collectivity, it constitutes the foundation or bed-rock of people's political behaviour and roles which, in turn, tend to influence significantly the pattern of performance of the Political System. Therefore, according to Almond,[10] the "pattern of political-culture" seems to be the most vital determinant of both micro-politics and macro-politics.

The relevance of "Political-Culture" for understanding political behaviour and roles of the individuals as well as the dynamics of the

Political System is also found to be greatly focused in the definitions and notions expressed by many other eminent scholars. For instance, Sidney Verba defines political-culture as "all politically relevant orientations.... orientations to all aspects of politics."[11] He explains, "The political culture of a society consists of the system of empirical beliefs, expressive symbols, and values which defines the situation in which political action takes place."[12] Verba further elaborates and points out: "As we use the term political culture, it refers to the system of beliefs about patterns of political interactions and institutions. It refers not to what is happening in the world of politics, but what people believe about these happenings. And these beliefs can be of several kinds: they can be empirical beliefs about what the actual state of political life is; they can be beliefs as to the goals or values that ought to be persued in political life, and these beliefs may have an important expressive or emotional dimension. Political culture forms an important link between the events of politics and the behaviour of individuals in reaction to those events......"[13] Thus, according to him, "political-culture" represents a system of control for individual's political interactions and for the working of political institutions as well.[14]

Similarly, Lucian W. Pye defines political-culture as the coherent pattern of individuals' "attitudes, sentiments, and cognitions that inform and govern political behaviour in any society....."[15] According to him, "For the individual the political culture provides controlling guidelines for effective political behaviour, and for the collectivity it gives a systematic structure of values and rational considerations which ensures coherence in the performance of institutions and organizations".[16] Pye, thus, asserts that the "political culture" which constitutes the psychological and subjective realm of politics gives meaning to the polity, form to the political process, discipline to political institutions, and relevance to individual's political acts.[17]

In a like manner, Fred I. Greenstein[18] conceptualizes political-culture as patterns of political orientations comprising the individuals' dispositions, beliefs, and attitudes towards political objects such as citizen-role, subject-role, and specialized-role in the Political System. Also Dennis Kavanagh[19] defines political-culture as "the emotional and attitudinal environment within which the political system operates."

Thus, conceptualizations and notions on "political-culture" are many and varied, and scholars have identified different objects or themes of political-culture. However, there may be noted a general consensus of opinions that the term "political-culture" refers to the individuals' patterns of political psychology which tend to condition significantly their political behaviour and roles, and also the performance of the Political System.

5.2 Classification of Political Culture

"Political-Culture", at the level of the individual and the collectivity may be empirically discerned and classified into different types and kinds. In this context, the proposition of Gabriel A. Almond and Sidney Verba seems to provide the most convenient and pragmatic guideline. Their proposition is presented in the pioneering work 'The Civic Culture' in which they opine: "The political culture of a nation is the particular distribution of patterns of orientation towards political objects among the members of the nation."[20] According to them, for discerning the patterns of political-culture and classifying them, the orientations of the individual towards political objects may be empirically enquired into, and analyzed. They point out that orientation comprises of the individual's 'cognition', 'affect', and 'evaluation'[21] towards an object or objects. 'Cognition' refers to the level of knowledge and awareness, accurate or otherwise, towards the object; whereas 'affect' refers to the feelings of attachment to or alienation from it, and 'evaluation' refers to the opinion and judgment of the individual on the concerned object as to whether it is good or bad, right or wrong, and just or unjust. Thus, there are three components of an orientation such as the cognitive component, the affective component, and the evaluative component which are to be enquired into, and ascertained in respect of political objects. As regard the political objects, there may be discerned four major categories[22] such as: (i) the National Political System as a general object, (ii) the Input-objects, (iii) the Output-objects, and (iv) the "Self" as an object in the political process of the Society. Towards each of these categories of political objects, the orientations of the individual in respect of cognition, affect, and evaluation are to be enquired into, and analyzed. For instance, the level of cognition of the individual, accurate or otherwise, in respect of the National Political System and its salient attributes such as its location, size, history, constitutional characteristics, etc. are to be enquired into. At the same time, enquires are to be undertaken for finding out the patterns of affect and evaluation of the individual towards his "National Political System" and its salient attributes. Similarly, enquires are also to be made for finding out, and ascertaining the patterns of cognition, affect and evaluation of the individual towards the "Input-objects" such as the process of interest-articulation and interest-aggregation undertaken by pressure-groups and political-parties, and also toward the "Output-objects" such as the process of rule-making, rule-application and rule-adjudication respectively undertaken by the legislature, the executive, and the judiciary. Moreover, the attitudinal patterns of the individual towards himself as political actor and his rights, duties and roles; and also his sense of "political-competence and efficacy" should be enquired into, and analyzed.

Such an exploration of the particular distribution of patterns of orientations in respect of cognition, affect, and evaluation towards the four major categories of political-objects such as the National Political System, the Input-objects, the Output-objects, and the Self as an object may facilitate empirical characterization of "political-culture" at the level of the individual, and at the level of the collectivity as well. Basing on the findings of these empirical investigations, as proposed by Gabriel A. Almond and Sidney Verba, "Political-Culture" may be classified into three pure types[23] such as: (i) Parochial Political Culture, (ii) Subject Political Culture, and (iii) Participant Political Culture.

5.2.1 Pure Types of Political Culture

The defining attributes of the "Pure Types" of "Political-Culture" are presented and symbolically illustrated in the table given below:

Pure Types of Political Culture[24]

Types of Political Culture	*Patterns of Orientation towards Political objects*			
	The National Political System	*Input-objects*	*Output-objects*	*Self as an object*
Parochial Political Culture	0	0	0	0
Subject Political Culture	1	0	1	0
Participant Political Culture	1	1	1	1

"Parochial Political Culture" represents the pattern of political-culture of an individual whose orientations to all the four major categories of political-objects approach zero. Such an individual does not have cognition, affect, and evaluation towards his National Political System, its input and output objects, and also towards himself as a political actor, and thus, he is not at-all oriented towards these political objects. He may be termed as 'the parochial individual' as he remains unaware of his National Political System and its political process, and does not play any role in it. As distinguished from the "Parochial Political Culture", the "Subject Political Culture" represents the pattern of political orientations of an individual who is oriented, in respect of cognition, affect, and evaluation, only towards his 'National Political System' and its 'Output-objects', but his orientations towards the 'Input-objects' and the 'Self' as an actor in the political process approach zero. The "subject individual", not being oriented toward the input-objects and himself as a political actor, does not make demands upon his Political System; and lacking in a sense of political competence and efficacy, he does not participate actively in its political process. He, thus, forms essentially a passive relationship with his Political System as he simply renders obedience to the latter. As different from the "Subject Political Culture", the "Participant Political Culture" represents the pattern of political orientations of an individual who is explicitly oriented, in respect of cognition, affect, and evaluation, towards all the four major categories of political objects such as his National Political System, its input-objects, output-objects, and towards himself as an active political actor. The participant individual forms accurate cognition of these political objects, and he is also distinctly oriented towards them in respect of affect and evaluation in the sense that he is either attached to or alienated from them, and he evaluates them either favourably or unfavourably. He, also, possesses a high sense of political-competence and efficacy as he feels himself competent to influence the decision-making process of his polity, and hence, he is oriented towards an activist role of the "Self" in the political process.

This three-fold classification of "Political-Culture", according to Almond and Verba, however, represents ideal types, and also presupposes that one type does not replace the other types.[25] For instance, the "Subject Political Culture" does not eliminate parochial and diffuse orientations to his primary social structures such as the family, and his identity in respect of social attributes such as race, ethnicity, caste, tribe, religion and language etc. Similarly, the "Participant Political Culture" is an additional stratum that may be added to, and combined with the subject and the parochial orientations. Thus, in reality, there may be noted the phenomenon of 'Cultural-mix"[26] at the level of both the individual and the collectivity. Therefore, the pattern of political-culture of the individual, in reality, may represent a mixture of parochial, subject, and participant orientations. However, these three types of orientations may be combined in the individual's psychology in different extent, and intensity. Of course, there may be discerned the predominance of one type of orientation as compared to the other types in the individual's psychology, and accordingly, the pattern of his "political-culture" may be empirically characterized. For instance, if the participant-orientation is predominant as compared to the subject and the parochial orientations, the individual's political culture may be characterized as the "participant political-culture" and he may be termed as the "participant-individual". Similarly, if in the individual, the "subject-orientations" predominate, he may be termed as the "subject-individual", and if in him, the "parochial-orientations" predominate, he may be termed as the "parochial-individual".

The phenomenon of 'Cultural-mix' may also be noticed, in reality, at the level of the mass or collectivity of the people of a Society. The population may consist of "the participant, the subject, and the parochial individuals" in different numerical sizes; and accordingly, the over-all pattern of "Political-Culture" that characterizes the people of a Society may be empirically discerned and typified. Therefore, in view of the phenomenon of 'Cultural-mix' at the level of the people of a Society, Almond and Verba classify the "Societal Political Culture" into four "Systemically mixed" types[27] such as: (i) the Parochial-Subject Political Culture, (ii) the Subject-Participant Political Culture, (iii) the Parochial-Participant Political Culture, and (iv) the Civic Culture.

5.2.2 Systemically-Mixed Types of Political Culture

The "Parochial-Subject Political-Culture" characterizes the people of a Society where most of the individuals are parochials, yet a segment of its population is found to have formed "subject-orientations" in the sense that they are only oriented towards the Centralized Political System and its output-objects. The pattern of political-culture of the people of the erstwhile Ottoman Empire of the medieval-age seems to provide an example of the type. As distinguished from the "Parochial-Subject Political-Culture", the "Subject-Participant Political-Culture" characterizes the people of a Society where most of its people have already formed the subject-orientations, yet a small segment of its population is found to have acquired and developed in them the participant-orientations in the sense that they tend to participate actively in the national political process. However, this participant-oriented stratum of the population may remain democratic aspirants only either because of lack of participant-structures such as parties, and pressure-groups and a free electoral system or because of frequent suspension of these structures by the 'Authoritarian Rulers'. The types of political-culture of the people of France, Italy, and Germany in the Nineteenth Century seem to provide examples of it. As different from this type, the "Parochial-Participant Political-Culture" characterizes the people of a Society where participant-structures such as parties, pressure-groups, and free electoral system have already been introduced, yet most of its people are found to retain very strong parochial allegiances to primordial institutions such as racial, ethnic, caste, tribal, religious, and language groups that tend to affect adversely their participant roles in the National Political System. They tend to uphold and promote parochial and primordial interests as and when these come into conflict with the national interests, and consequently, the "National Participant Structures" become unable to function democratically in the true sense of the term. This type of political-culture seems to characterize the people of most of the "New Nations" that have emerged in Asia, Africa, Latin-America, and the Middle-East in the post Second World War period. Those new States which are democratic in form and have introduced participant political structures are found to suffer from chronic political instability and disorder because most of the people of these States play their participant political roles under heavy pressure of parochial and primordial allegiances that are upheld and promoted at the cost of national interest.

As distinguished from the above three types, the "Civic Culture"[28] is characterized by a fine blending and harmonious synthesis of the participant, the subject, and the parochial orientations in the psychology of the individual. The "civic-individual" tends to be actively involved in the political process of his National Political System. As a conscious citizen, he makes demands upon his Political System on varieties of societal issues keeping always in view the national interest, and ventilates the demands peacefully through political parties, pressure-groups, mass-media, public meetings and other democratic agencies and avenues. He possesses a high sense of political competence and efficacy, and tends to influence the process of public policy-making. He regularly votes at the elections, attends and organizes public meetings, undertakes election campaigns, and also contests at the elections. He, thus, actively participates in the political process, and, of course, all his political participatory activities are based on reason and national interest as he tends to be rational and national in his approach to politics. However, his 'participant' political orientations combine with, but do not replace, his subject and parochial orientations.[29] Even though he is an active participant in the political process, he renders obedience to the authoritative decisions, policies, and laws of his Political System, and simultaneously, he retains parochial allegiance to his primordial institutions such as racial, ethnic, tribal, caste, religious, language groups etc. However, his parochial allegiance does not conflict with his allegiance to the National Political System as he is prepared to sacrifice or subdue his parochial allegiance for upholding national interest. Thus, the "Civic Culture" is "an allegiant participant culture"[30] that orients the individual positively to both the "input" and "output" structures and process, and represents a balanced fusion[31] of political activity, rationality, national allegiance with reverence for traditions, and with commitment to parochial values as well. Empirical evidences of the "Civic Culture" may be noticed, in the contemporary time, in the developed Political Societies such as the U.K. and the U.S.A.

These various types of systemically-mixed political-culture represent the over-all patterns of political orientations of the people of different National Societies, and each of these tends to condition not only the political behaviour of the people but also the performance or the dynamics of its Political System. Hence, it is the type of "Political Culture" of the people of a National Society that constitutes the foundation of its Political System, and that also becomes, most likely, the vital determinant of its structure or form as well as political stability and viability. Therefore, an enquiry into, and analysis of "Culture-Structure Relationship" may become necessary for comprehending the dynamics of the Political System of a Society.

5.3 Culture-Structure Relationship

There may be discerned, following Almond's proposition, three distinct types of relationship between the type of "Political-Culture" of the people of a Society, and the "Structure or Form" of their Political System. These three types[32] are: (i) Relationship of Allegiance, (ii) Relationship of Apathy, and (iii) Relationship of Alienation; and each of them is characterized by distinct patterns of orientations in respect of cognition, affect, and evaluation of the people toward the above-mentioned four major types of political objects conjointly. These are presented and symbolically illustrated in the following Table:

Types of Culture-Structure Relationship

Over-all pattern of orientation towards political objects	*Types of Relationship*		
	Allegiance	*Apathy*	*Alienation*
Cognitive Orientation	+	+	+
Affective Orientation	+	0	-
Evaluation Orientation	+	0	-

The relationship between the pattern of "Political-Culture" of the people, and "Structure" of the Political System of a Society may be termed as the "Relationship of Allegiance"[33] or congruence if political cognition in the population, in general, would tend to be accurate, and political affect and evaluation would tend to be favourable as illustrated by the plus (+) or positive symbols. On the contrary, if the Political System and other political objects are simply cognized by the people, in general, but their 'affect' and 'evaluation' towards them approach indifference or zero, the type of the "Culture-Structure Relationship" may be termed as the "Relationship of Apathy".[34] However, incongruence or alienation between the pattern of "Political-Culture" of the people and the "Structure" of the Political System seems to begin when the point of indifference is crossed, and negative political affect and evaluation are formed in the population. Hence, if cognition towards the Political system and other political objects becomes accurate, but their "affect" and "evaluation" towards these objects become negative, the type of "Culture-Structure Relationship" may be termed as the "Relationship of Alienation".[35]

These three types of "Culture-Structure Relationship" tend to determine the prospect of stability, or instability and transformation of a Political System. "Allegiant" or congruent relationship would, most likely, facilitate and ensure stability and viability of the Political System; whereas 'Apathetic Relationship' signals for, and initiates the process of political instability; and 'Alienated Relationship' brings about, and culminates in political change and transformation.[36]

5.4 Political Culture and Political Dynamics

Thus, "Political-Culture" seems to be the most vital determinant of political behaviour and roles of the individuals as well as the dynamics of the Political System. It helps us to understand and explain as to why the individual behaves the way he behaves in the political arena, and also why the Political System works the way it works. For the individual, the pattern of his "Political-Culture" that characterizes his psychology tends to shape and mould his political behaviour and roles; and for the Political System, the pattern of "Political-Culture" of the people, in general, tends to influence the content and style of its performance, and to determine the prospect of its stability, viability, and modernity as well.[37] The Political System is likely to remain stable and viable provided its 'Structure' is congruent with, and allegiant to the pattern of "Political-Culture" of its people, and also, it is likely to acquire and display the attributes modernity[38] provided the pattern of "Political-Culture" of its people becomes 'the Civic Culture' characterized by allegiant, participant, rational, pragmatic, national, and secular orientations. Therefore, the discernment and analysis of the pattern of "Political-Culture" at the level of the individual and the mass of people seem to provide meaningful insights for understanding and appreciating both micro-politics and macro-politics in a Society, and also the process of its political modernization and development.

REFERENCES

1. Edward B. Taylor, Quoted by Milton Singer in 'Culture' in David. L. Sills (ed.), *International Encyclopedia of Social Sciences*. (New York: The Macmillan & the Free Press, 1968) Vol. III, p. 527.
2. Raymond W. Firth, *Elements of Social Organization*. (London. Watts, 1961), p. 27.
3. E.K. Wilson, *Sociology: Rules, Roles and Relationships*. (Illinois: Dorsey Press, 1966), p. 51.
4. Gabriel A. Almond and Sidney Verba, *The Civic Culture*. (Princeton, N.J.: Princeton University Press, 4th Printing, 1972), p. 14. Originally published by the Princeton University Press, Princeton, N.J. (U.S.A.) in 1963.
5. Marvin E. Olsen, *The Process of Social Organization* (New Delhi: Oxford and IBH Publishing Co., 1975), p. 62. Originally published by Holt, Rinehart & Winston, New York in 1968.
6. Gabriel A. Almond, 'Comparative Political System'. *The Journal of Politics*, Vol. 18, No. 3, 1956 p. 396.
7. Gabriel A. Almond, 'A Functional Approach to Comparative Politics' in Gabriel A. Almond and James S. Coleman (eds), *The Politics of the Developing Areas*. (Princeton, N.J.: Princeton University Press, Paperback Edn, 1970), pp. 27-28. Originally published by the Princeton University Press, Princeton, N.J., USA in 1960.
8. Gabriel A. Almond, *The Civic Culture, Op. cit.*, p. 14.
9. *Ibid.*, pp. 32-33.
10. *Ibid.*, pp. 32-33.
11. Sidney Verba, 'Comparative Political Culture' in Lucian W. Pye & Sidney Verba (eds.), *Political Culture and Political Development*. (Princeton, N.J.: Princeton University Press, Paperback Edn, 1969), pp. 518. Originally published by the Princeton University Press, Princeton, N.J., USA in 1965.
12. *Ibid.*, p. 513.
13. *Ibid.*, p. 516.
14. *Ibid.*, p. 517.
15. Lucian W. Pye, 'Political Culture and Political Development' in Lucian W. Pye and Sidney Verba (eds), *Political Culture and Political Development op. cit.*, p. 7.
16. *Ibid.*, p. 7.
17. *Ibid.*, p. 7.
18. Fred I. Greenstein, 'Political Socialization' in David L. Sills (ed) *International Encylopedia of the Social Sciences*. (New York: The Macmillan and the Free Press, 1968) Vol. 14, p. 552.

19. Dennis Kavanagh, *Political Culture*. (London: The Macmillan Press, 1972) p. 10.
20. Gabriel A. Almond and Sidney Verba, *The Civic Culture*. *Op. cit.*, pp. 14-15.
21. *Ibid*., p. 15.
22. *Ibid*., p. 15.
23. *Ibid*., p. 17, p. 17, and also, p. 23.
24. *Ibid*., p. 17.
25. *Ibid*., p. 19.
26. *Ibid*., p. 20.
27. *Ibid*., pp. 22-23.
28. *Ibid*., p. 31.
29. *Ibid*., p. 31.
30. *Ibid*., p. 31.
31. *Ibid*., p. 32.
32. *Ibid*., p. 22.
33. *Ibid*., pp. 21-22.
34. *Ibid*., p. 22.
35. *Ibid*., p. 22.
36. *Ibid*., p. 21.
37. *Ibid*., p. 33.
38. *Ibid*., p. 504. Also Gabriel A. Almond and G.B. Powell, Jr, *Comparative Politics: A Developmental Approach*. (New Delhi: American Polishing Co., Indian Reprint, 1975), p. 63, Originally published by Little Brown and Company, Boston, USA, in 1966.

6

Political Socialization

6.1 The Concept

The term "Political Socialization" ordinarily connotes 'Socialization in Politics'. Therefore, it seems imperative to discern the meaning of the term 'socialization' and its scope and implications. The term 'socialization' is defined as the process of social-learning through which 'societal-culture' is learned and imbibed. In the process of 'socialization', the individuals learn social values, norms, and beliefs, what may be broadly termed as 'societal culture', and consequently, their 'social orientations' and 'social-self'[1] are formed. Their social orientations and dispositions, as formed through the process of socialization, shape their behaviour and social roles which, in turn, tend to determine the dynamics of the Society as well as the prospect of societal stability or change. Therefore, for successful attainment of the goal of societal stability and viability, three major tasks such as: (i) enculturation, (ii) impulse-control, and (iii) role-training are sought to be performed through the process of socialization.[2] Enculturation involves socialization of the individuals in the 'societal-culture', through intra-generational and inter-generational transmission; impulse-control involves education of the individual for curbing his disruptive tendencies, and channelizing them in socially acceptable directions; and role-training involves training of the individual for performing socially acceptable roles. Successful performance of these three tasks through the process of socialization would enable the Society to attain and maintain its stability and viability.

'Socialization' is, thus, a comprehensive process of social learning, and when it takes place in the political context, and is involved with the political learning of the individuals, it may be termed as the process of "Political Socialization". As such, "Political Socialization" is the process through which the individuals learn political values, norms, and beliefs, and as a consequence, 'political culture' is formed in them. It is this pattern of political-culture as formed in them through the process of "Political Socialization" that tends to determine the content and style of their political behaviour and roles. Simultaneously, the pattern of political behaviour of the people as conditioned by the over-all pattern of their political-culture tends to influence significantly the performance and dynamics of the Political System of the Society.

The relevance of the 'political-socialization phenomenon' as the process of political learning with determinative consequences for the political behaviour of the individual and the dynamics of the Political System has drawn interest and attention of both scholars and statesmen, from the time of commencement of political existence of man-kind, even though the term has been coined in recently. To mention precisely, the credit for the coinage of this term may be accorded to Herbert H. Hyman who, through his pioneering work 'Political Socialization: A Study in the Psychology of Political behaviour'[3] published in 1959, has drawn scholarly interest, in contemporary time, to the 'political-socialization phenomenon' as a renewed and vital area of study and research. From the time of publication of this work of Hyman, more and more scholars and researchers have become concerned with the study and analysis of the 'political-socialization phenomenon', though scholarly differences are noticed in their notions and views on its meaning, approaches, and scope.

The following definitions and notions on 'Political Socialization' advocated by some renowned scholars deserve attention and analysis.

Fred I. Greenstein: Political socialization encompasses all political learning, formal and informal, deliberate and unplanned, at every stage of the life-cycle, including not only explicitly political learning but also nominally non-political learning of politically relevant personality characteristics."[4]

Richard E. Dawson and Kenneth Prewitt: Political

socialization process operates at both the individual and community levels. At the community level, it is best understood as cultural transmission,[5] whereas at the level of the individual, it refers to "the developmental processes through which the citizen matures politically, and acquires a complex of beliefs, feelings, and information which help him comprehend, evaluate, and relate to the political world around him."[6]

Harry Eckstein: Political Socialization refers to the "processes through which values, cognitions, and symbols are learned and internalized, through which operative social norms regarding politics are implanted, political roles institutionalized, and political consensus created, either effectively or ineffectively."[7]

Gabriel A. Almond: "Political socialization is the process of induction into the political culture."[8] By means of it, "all political systems tend to perpetuate their cultures and structures through time."[9]

David Easton and Jack Dennis: Political Socialization consists of those developmental processes through which individuals acquire political orientations and patterns of behaviour.[10] It "contributes to the capacity of a political system to persist in a world either of stability or change."[11]

An analysis of these notions and views reveals that 'political-socialization' is essentially the process of political learning that operates at the level of the individual as well the collectivities or the mass of people. Through this process, the individual learns political orientations as well as politically relevant non-political orientations; and consequently, the pattern of his 'political-culture' is formed and shaped. Moreover, through this process, there takes place political learning of the collectivities and the mass of people of the Society, and as a consequence, the pattern of 'societal political culture' is formed. Therefore, on help-forming the patterns of 'political-culture' of the individual and the collectivities, it tends to condition significantly not only the individual's political behaviour and roles but also the people's political roles which, in turn, determines the over-all performance of the Political System. However, as regard its consequences for, and implications upon the dynamics of the Political System, the visions and views of scholars may be discerned into two perspectives such as: (i) the systemic-maintenance perspective, and (ii) the systemic-persistence perspective. The chief proponent of the 'systemic-maintenance' perspective is Gabriel A. Almond[12] who considers "political socialization" as a vital functional process through which the people of a Political System are made to learn, and inducted into the congruent pattern of 'political-culture' that sustains, maintains, and nourishes it. Consequently, because of cultural-structural congruence, the Political System is enabled to maintain its structure or form intact, and to remain stable and viable through time as well. On the contrary, the chief advocate of the 'systemic-persistence' perspective is David Easton[13] who considers "political socialization" as a major functional process through which the people of a Society may learn and develop different patterns of political orientations and dispositions, but they, at the minimum, are socialized to display generalized or diffuse-support towards the Political System which, as a consequence, is enabled to undertake authoritative allocation of values for the Society, and to persist[14] through time. Hence, the "political socialization process" contributes toward the persistence or survival of the Political System, even though radical as well as frequent changes may occur in its norms and forms.

Thus, these two perspectives focus on different and divergent goals that are sought to be attained through the "political socialization process". The 'systemic-maintenance' perspective asserts that 'political socialization' is exclusively involved with the task of effective attainment of the goal of 'maintenance' of the Political System intact on inducting the people into the congruent pattern of 'political-culture', and also on preventing occurrence of vital change in the prevalent structure of the Political System; whereas the 'systemic-persistence' perspective identifies 'persistence' of the Political System as the ultimate goal to be attained through the "political socialization process", and is unconcerned, with vital changes that may be brought about in the norms and forms of the Political System. However, these two divergent perspectives should be combined in view of the realities of political life because every Political System incessantly strives to maintain political stability in the sense of stability its form or over-all structure but is constrained to bring about political changes as and when these become necessary for its very survival. Hence, in view of the quest for political stability, and the inevitability of political changes, "political-socialization" ought to be perceived not merely as a vital functional process concerned with the maintenance of the Political System but also as a major functional mechanism that contributes toward political change and transformation. What is required, therefore, is a combined perspective "which is not only includes the possibility that socialization contributes to stability but which also recognizes that change itself may be an equally frequent outcome of socialization."[15]

6.2 Forms of Political Socialization

Through the process of 'political socialization', the individual tends to learn and acquire patterns of political orientations and dispositions. As such, it involves interactions between the 'socializer' and the 'socializee' because political learning is essentially an "interaction-acquisition process".[16] However, political learning of the individual may take place through various forms and modes, and these may be classified into two broad categories such as: (i) Manifest Form and (ii) Latent Form.[17]

6.2.1 Manifest Form

'Manifest Political Socialization' involves transmission of explicitly political orientations by the political-socializers, and the learning of these orientations by the socializee. However, the socializer may transmit explicitly political orientations intentionally or un-intentionally, and the socializee may learn these through various methods and modes, such as: (i) Imitation, (ii) Anticipatory Political Socialization, (iii) Political Experiences, and (iv) Political Education.[18]

The socializee may imitate political ideas and values of those persons whom he considers as the 'model', and gets politically socialized accordingly even if these explicitly political orientations are not being transmitted intentionally by the socializer. For instance, a child may learn the political values of his father or his teacher on observing their party-allegiance or preference, commitment to political ideology, allegiance to the nation-state etc. Similarly, un-intentional manifest political-socialization may take place through the method of 'anticipatory political-socialization' when the socializee, in anticipation of holding a political position in future, may learn the required political mannerisms and dispositions. For instance, an aspirant for membership of the legislature may learn political orientations that are appropriate to it much before he, in reality, becomes its member. Also, un-intentional manifest political-socialization may take place through the method of 'political experience' when the socializee tends to learn political orientations through experiences incurred in the political process. As distinguished from these methods of un-intentional manifest political socialization, intentional manifest political-socialization may take place through the method of 'political education'. For instance, political parties may intentionally undertake endeavours to educate the people in their respective political ideologies through campaigns and public meetings.

6.2.2 Latent Form

'Latent Political Socialization' involves transmission of non-political orientations with potential political consequences that help-form the individual's political-self and his political orientations. However, 'latent political-socialization' of the individual may be intentionally or unintentionally undertaken by the socializee in various methods and modes such as: (i) Inter-personal transference, (ii) Apprenticeship, and (iii) Generalizations.[19]

'Inter-personal transference' involves both intentional and un-intentional transmission of politically relevant non-political orientations by the socializer to the socializee, and it takes place because of inter-personal relationship between them. For instance, parents may intentionally instruct the child to become a good boy on rendering unquestioning obedience to the orders of the elders in the family, and the child, because of this regular and intimate inter-personal relationship with the parents, may easily and quickly learn this authoritarian value that may subsequently influence him to form his political-self and dispositions imbuing with authoritarian attributes. Moreover, through inter-personal transference, the socializer may undertake latent political socialization of the socializee un-intentionally. For instance, a school-student may imbibe 'authority-orientations' corresponding to his teacher's authority-pattern, whether democratic or authoritarian, and subsequently, his political dispositions and politically relevant personality-traits may be accordingly shaped, even if no deliberate endeavour is made by the teacher in this context.

Apart from 'Inter-personal transference' as a mode, 'latent political socialization' may take place through the method of 'Apprenticeship' that involves learning of specific skills and expertise in the process of performing roles in social situations. This non-political learning of the socializee undertaken, whether deliberately or non-deliberately by the socializer, tends to condition his political behaviour and roles. For instance, participatory experiences and skills learned by the socializee in the family, the peer-group, and the work-place may make him an active participant in the political process.

Moreover, 'latent political socialization' may take place through the mode of 'generalization' that involves the process of motivating the socializee to generalize his societal culture, values and beliefs, and to extend these to the political arena. For instance, if the 'culture' or belief-system of the people of a Society imbues with the attribute of fatalism, their political orientations would, most likely, be characterized by it, and they may view the Government as well as the political process with fatalistic resignation, even if the Government misrules, or the political process becomes vitiated with injustice and corruption.

Thus, there are various modes and methods of both latent, and manifest political socialization through which political learning of the socializee may be undertaken. However, as these modes and methods are many and varied, and as political learning is a complex psychological process, it may become difficult to ascertain, accurately and precisely, the form and the mode through which the individual gets politically socialized.

6.3 Political Socializers

Political learning of the individual takes place as a consequence of his exposure to, and interactions with various "Political-Socializers" or agents of political-socialization at different stages of his life such as childhood, adolescence, and adulthood. In this life-long process of learning, political-socializers tend to transmit explicitly political orientations as well as politically relevant non-political orientations to the individual and that too, intentionally or non-intentionally. As such, they contribute significantly to the formation of the individual's 'political-self', and the pattern of his 'political-culture'. Thus, political-socialization of the individual takes place under the aegis of many and varied political-socializers. However, there may be discerned some universal and very important political-socializers such as family, school, peer-group, mass-media, secondary-groups, and the political-process that seem to play crucial roles in the context of political-socialization of the individual at different stages of his life.

6.3.1 Family

Among the 'political-socializers', family occupies a place of paramount importance as it is the first socializer to write on the empty political slate of the individual during his childhood when the child tends to form his initial orientations and belief-system. The child is not only born in the family but also is reared up in its environment from birth till adolescence. During these formative years of his life, the child becomes completely dependent upon the family, especially his parents, for satisfaction of basis needs such as food, clothes, shelter, safety, and also love, and affection. Parents not only provide these basis needs to him, but they also dispense rewards for approved behaviour, and punishment for disobedience. Therefore, the child tends to view his parents as the model or significant persons, and he feels induced to perform gratification-eliciting activities.[20] Moreover, the child's emotional attachment with his parents, and his regular informal interactions with them create the most congenial environment for the child who tends to imitate and acquire parental values, beliefs, orientations and dispositions easily. As James C. Davies emphatically points outs: ".... The family provides the major means for transforming the mentally naked infant organism into the adult, fully clothed in its own personality. And most of the individual's political personality—his tendencies to think and act politically in particular ways—have been determined at home several years before he can take part in politics as an ordinary citizen or as a political prominent."[21] Thus, family may contribute immensely toward the individual's political learning during his childhood, and hence, it seems to have tremendous potentiality to play crucial roles in the context of both latent and manifest political-socialization of the child.

Family may undertake latent political-socialization of the child deliberately as well as inadvertently or non-deliberately. It may directly and deliberately transmit to the child some non-political values and orientations which may, later on, be politically relevant during his adulthood in conditioning his political roles and behaviour. In this context, an interesting example is parental instructions issued to the child for performing gender-appropriate roles that may subsequently result in passivity for woman and activeness for man in the sphere of politics. The female-child is usually instructed by the parents to remain indoor, and to help her mother in house-keeping activities; whereas the male-child is encouraged by the parents to remain active in out-door activities, and to play leadership roles. Such deliberate instructions issued by the parents to the children for performing gender-appropriate roles may produce long-lasting consequences in conditioning their mind-set, and behaviour accordingly, and in making females usually less active and less interested than males in the realm of Politics.[22]

In the context of latent political-socialization of the child, family may transmit inadvertently or non-deliberately some important non-political orientations that may have subsequent political implications for his political behaviour during adulthood. For instance, the child, by virtue of his membership in the family, comes to learn its social identities and attributes in respect of race, ethnicity, caste, tribe, language, religion, class etc. These social identities may serve as important referral variables[23] for his political behaviour and roles during adulthood. Moreover, the "Parental Authority-Structure",[24] even if it is non-political in content, tends to contribute significantly towards the formation of the child's personality that may be subsequently relevant in conditioning his political behaviour. For instance, "parental authority-structure", whether authoritarian or democratic in essence, may shape the child's personality in the corresponding pattern. The "parental authority-structure" may be characterized as the 'Authoritarian pattern'[25] if parents administer rigid discipline on the child, do not allow him to participate in the family decision-making process, and demand unquestioning obedience to their decisions and orders; whereas it may be characterized as the 'Democratic-pattern'[26] if parents treat the child with affection and friendliness, and encourage and allow him to participate in the family decision-making process. In case of the 'Authoritarian pattern' of the 'parental authority-structure', the child, because of his regular interactions with parents, is, most likely, to learn authoritarian values and orientations, and to form an 'authoritarian personality' characterized by 'dominance-submissiveness'[27] tendency. On the contrary, regular interactions of the child with parents characterized by the 'democratic-authority-structure' may infuse in him participant orientations, and may help-form the 'democratic personality' in him. The child's learning of the 'authority-orientations', and the consequent formation of his personality corresponding to his 'parental authority-structure', whether democratic or authoritarian in form and essence, may significantly condition his subsequent political behaviour during adulthood, and may make him correspondingly either an authoritarian or a democratic actor in the political arena.

Besides 'latent political-socialization', the family may also undertake 'manifest political-socialization' of the child. In this context, it may transmit to the child, deliberately as well as non-deliberately, explicitly political orientations and values.[28] Parents and other members of the family may, among themselves, discuss on public policies, laws, role of political leaders and the ministers, activities of the government and public officials, ideologies and role of political parties, electoral process, and political events etc. These discussions on political and public affairs in the family may communicate explicitly political orientations, values and preferences to the child, and consequently, the political learning of the child may take place.[29] The child may directly and actively participate in these discussions or he may over-hear them, and consequently, his manifest political socialization may take place either deliberately or non-deliberately.

Thus, the family may play a crucial role in the context of both manifest and latent political-socialization of the child; and it may cast a deep and enduring imprint on his political learning. However, its role as a political socializer seems to be confined mostly to the child's latent political-socialization because of cognitive immaturity of the child to comprehended explicitly political orientations and values.

6.3.2 School

The school is the first public institution, beyond the family-environment, with which the child comes into contact during the pre-adult phase of his life that extends from his childhood to adolescence. It is in the school that he gets formal education and instructions imparted by the teachers in a wide variety of ideas, values, and skills on the basis of a deliberately framed syllabus. However, in the school, he not only learns formal curricular instructions, but also interacts regularly with teachers and fellow school-mates, and participates in extra-curricular activities as well. All these curricular instructions as well as extra-curricular experiences acquired by him during school-years when he gradually matures from childhood to adolescence tend to shape, to a great extent, his politically relevant self. Thus, the school seems to have tremendous potentiality to play its role as a 'political-socializer', and it may undertake both manifest, and latent political-socialization of the student through some major agencies and mechanisms such as the curriculum, the teacher, the school-rituals, the school social-milieu, and the school extra-curricular activities.[30]

The school-curriculum may serve as a major instrument through which manifest and deliberate political-socialization of the student may take place. It may be so designed as to imbue with preferred political values, and these may be directly learned and acquired by the student when teaching is imparted by the teacher on the basis of the curriculum in the class-room. For instance, courses in national history may highlight periods of national glory only; and courses in civics and government may glorify the existing regime and its political ideology. Thus, it is through the school-curriculum that civic-education or political indoctrination of the students may be undertaken; and an allegiant and integrated citizenry may be created[31] by way of educating them directly in the desired political values and orientations.

As formal instructions and teachings are imparted to the students in the class-room by the teacher, the latter may exert considerable influence upon the former in the process of formation of their political-self. The teacher may undertake manifest political-socialization of the students by way of teaching them in explicitly political values and ideas as contained in the curriculum. However, the government-school teacher, being a government servant, usually limits his teachings to consensual and pro-regime political values; whereas the non-government school-teacher may transmit partisan political values and ideas to the students through formal instructions in the class-room.

Apart from manifest political-socialization, the teacher may also contribute toward latent political-socialization of the students. In this, context, the teacher, by way of acting as the 'Authority figure' in the class-room, deliberately instructs the students on some non-political values such as values of maintenance of discipline and order, and obedience to school-rules and regulations which may later on be relevant in shaping their political behaviour and roles. Moreover, the teacher may non-deliberately and inadvertently contribute towards formation of the politically relevant personality-traits of the students. In this context, 'the Authority-structure' of the teacher, whether democratic or authoritarian in form and essence, seems to be a crucial determinant.[32] The teacher's 'Authority-structure' may be characterized as the 'Democratic pattern' if the teacher interacts with the students with warmth and affection, and allows and encourages them to participate actively in the process of curricular discussions in the class-room[33]. On the contrary, if the teacher is very strict and rigid in his relationship with the students, gives severe punishment even for minor acts of indiscipline, and does not permit them to participate actively in curricular discussions, his 'Authority-structure' may be characterized as the 'Authoritarian Pattern'.[34] The teacher's 'Authority-structure', characterized whether by democratic or authoritarian traits, tends to transmit corresponding orientations to the students who may inadvertently learn these, and form their personality accordingly. The personality of the students, thus formed as a consequence of the indirect influence of the 'Teachers Authority-Structure' may, later on, be politically relevant in conditioning their political roles and interactions.

Besides the teacher and the curriculum, the school may undertake political-socialization of the students through observance of national rituals and ceremoinies[35] such as hoisting of National Flag and singing of National Anthem in nationally relevant occasions, and payment of respect and honour to the national symbols and leaders. The observance of these national rituals and ceremonies may inculcate in the students a sense of patriotism and legitimacy toward the Political System, and hence, may contribute towards their manifest political-socialization.

The school may also provide for latent political socialization of the students through organization and conduct of extra-curricular activities[36] such as games, sports, athletic competitions, debate competitions, and cultural functions etc. In participating in the extra-curricular activities sponsored and organized by the school, the students may learn, inadvertently, participatory values, and develop a sense of self-efficacy and competence that may help-form participant personality in them, and may make them participant political actors during adulthood.

Moreover, in the context of latent political-socialization of the student, the school social-milieu or social climate[37] may play a determining role. The social-composition of the student-population in terms of race, ethnicity, language, gender, caste, religion, and class etc. may, inadvertently, instill in the students some politically relevant values and attitudes. For instance, homogeneous social-milieu in the school may inculcate in the students values of group-identification and discrimination; whereas heterogeneous social-composition of the student-population may help-form values of inter-group co-operation and harmony in the students. These values of discrimination and conflict, or co-operation and harmony as learned by the students may be subsequently relevant for them in forming their perception and vision of the political society, and performing their political roles accordingly.

Thus, the school may undertake both manifest and latent political-socialization of the students through school-life. However, the role the school as an effective political-socializer seems to be crucially affected by the newness or the redundancy of the values and orientations transmitted by it. The school is likely to exert significant influence upon the students if their socialization experiences under the aegis of the school are not redundant but new. In case, the school transmits such values and orientations in which the students have already seen socialized through the agency of the family, it is less likely to exert independent impact upon them. Of course, the redundancy or repetition of values and orientations which the school transmits may serve to reinforce the earlier socialization experiences of the students.

6.3.3 Peer-Group

Peer-group refers to "a form of primary group composed of members sharing relatively equal status and intimate ties".[38] It is also known as "informal face-to-face group".[39] These groups may be formed, and informal membership in them may be acquired by the individual at different stages of his life such as childhood, adolescence, and adulthood. As the peer-group is characterized by informal, and emotional inter-personal relationship among age-homogeneous peers, and is without any authority-structure and authority-relationship, it may provide a congenial environment for both manifest and latent political-socialization of its members.[40] Its membership facilitates active participation of the peer in the peer-group activities, and hence, the peers may form in them participant orientations, and a high sense of self-efficacy which may subsequently be extended to the political arena, and may make them active participants in the political process.[41] Moreover, the peer-group may undertake manifest political-socialization of its members provided it is a politicized group characterized by a distinct political ideology and party-preference. Thus, factors such as the extent of politicization of the peer-group, the level of intimacy among the peers, regularity of interactions among them, and the degree of homogeneity in their values and orientations seem to determine its effectiveness as a political socializer.[42]

6.3.4 Mass-Media

Mass-media are the media for mass-communication such as Newspapers, Radio, Television, Books, Journals, Cinema etc. which disseminate information to the people at large. Because of their wide coverage of the socio-political scenario, and day-to-day dissemination of varieties of information including political information and non-political information, and also because of their easier, and quicker accessibility to a large audience, the mass-media may contribute significantly toward political-socialization of the individual.

Mass-media may undertake latent political-socialization of the individual trough transmission of non-political information and orientations. For instance, stories and articles in books and magazines; songs, music, and other non-political programme transmitted through the Radio, Television, Cinema; and even the advertisements made through these media for the sale of a product may contain non-political values and views which may become politically relevant in forming political values and dispositions of the socializee. Non-political values such as those of social harmony or conflict, cultural identification and discrimination or tolerance, localism or nationalism and patriotism, peace or violence etc. may be learned by the individual through media-exposure, and these non-political values, on being transferred and extended by him to the political arena, may condition his political orientations and behaviour accordingly. Therefore, the non-political communication-package of the mass-media, even though it is designed "merely to entertain the audience, or to sell a product and make money for a producer, may well serve the latent function of political socialization."[43]

Mass-media may also contribute significantly toward manifest political-socialization of the individual through transmission of explicitly political information, views, and values. For instance, news bulletins as transmitted by the Radio and the Television; and political news, views, and articles as published in the Newspapers, Magazines, and Journals not only provide political information to the individual but also help-form his political values and orientations directly.[44]

Thus, mass-media seem to have tremendous potentiality to contribute to the political learning of the individual. Of course, they tend to exert significant influence upon the socializee in re-socializing him in those values and orientations which are not deeply rooted in him; but in case of deeply rooted and held values and beliefs of the individual, mass-media seem to exert little or minimal influence because of the socializee's selective exposure, and selective perception of media-communication.[45]

6.3.5 Secondary Groups

Secondary-groups[46] are characterized by formal organization and distinct objectives which are sought to be realized through group-relevant activities of their members. These groups may be classified into two broad types such as political-groups, and non-political groups, and they may play important roles in the context of political-socialization of the individual.[47] Political secondary-groups, for instance political parties, mostly undertake manifest political socialization of the socializee by way of educating and indoctrinating him deliberately in their respective party-ideologies and policies through various modes such as public-meetings, discussions and debates, media-communications, and campaigns etc. On the contrary, non-political secondary-groups, for instance interest groups, attitude groups and varieties of pressure-groups which are characterized by non-political homogeneous objective, mostly undertake latent political-socialization of their members. The socializee, due to his membership in such groups, may participate actively in group-activities, and hence, may learn participant orientations and a sense of self-efficacy which may influence him to play active and participant roles in the political process.

Thus, secondary-groups, both political and non-political, may contribute significantly toward political-socialization of the socializee. Of course, their effectiveness as political socializers seems to be determined by the degree of closeness of the socializee to his group as well as the frequency of his participation in group-activities.

6.3.6 Political Process

Political-process of the Society may itself contribute significantly towards manifest political-socialization of the individual. It provides opportunities to him to gain direct political experiences through observation of or participation in various political events and occurrences such as elections, debates and discussions in the legislature, governmental decisions and policies, role of the political leaders, role of the bureaucrats and public officials, press-notes, public meetings, agitation, and socio-political movements etc. These direct political experiences obtained in the political process may acquaint him with political realities, and therefore, may "serve to correct or complete"[48] his political learning, and help-shape his political self accordingly. However, the political process may exert determinative influence upon those socializees who are politically active and attentive; whereas for those who are not interested in, and inattentive to politics, it is less likely to influence the formation of their political-self.[49]

6.3.7 Pre-Conditions of Agental-Influence

The extent of impact of the "Political-Socializers" or agents of political-socialization upon the socializee may be crucially determined by three major pre-conditions such as: (i) Exposure, (ii) Communication, and (iii) Receptivity.[50] Influence may be exerted by the agent or socializer upon the socializee only when the latter is exposed to the former. However, mere exposure of the socializee to the socializer may not ensure his political socialization. Along with 'exposure', the additional requirement is deliberate transmission of desired information or 'communication' by the socializer to the socializee. Moreover, effective political learning of the socializee tends to be determined by his 'receptivity' to the communication as transmitted by the socializer. Of course, the extent of the socializee's receptivity seems to depend upon his cognitive maturity, and also the degree of intensity of his emotional relationship with the socializer because the socializee may receive and internalize these communications effectively provided he understands them, and provided he is emotionally attached to the socializer. Thus, the role of the political-socializers in the process of political-socialization of the individual, and the extent of their impact upon the latter tend to be crucially determined by these three major pre-conditions such as 'exposure', 'communication', and 'receptivity'.

6.4 Sequence of Political Socialization

Thus, Political socialization which a life-long process of political-learning commences from the child-hood of the socializee, and continues through-out his life. However, as regard the sequence of political-socialization involving continuity of political learning or its change during adulthood in conformity with recent experiences, there may be discerned, as Robert Weissberg opines,[51] two different perspectives such as: (i) the Primacy-perspective, and (ii) the Recency-perspective. In this context, the 'Primacy perspective' postulates that basic political values, beliefs, and attitudes acquired by the socializee during his pre-adulthood are relatively more enduring through-out life, and these tend to determine significantly his political orientations and dispositions during adulthood. As Dawson and Prewitt emphatically point out: "........political learning is cumulative. Orientations learned early in life determine much of the form and substance of orientations acquired later."[52]

As distinguished from it, the 'Recency perspective' postulates that political orientations of the individual are malleable and changeable throughout his life-cycle, and that the closer a learning experience to the adulthood, the greater is its influence upon the socializee. The rationale of this perspective derives from the fact that Politics is the domain of the adults, not of the children, and that it involves learning of complex concepts and skills which may not be comprehended by the children but may be cognized and learned by the adults. Therefore, recent socialization-experiences tend to condition his political orientations firmly, and as Dean Jaros emphatically points outs: ".....early socialization may be displaced, or overridden by later socialization, nullified by later experiences......"[53]

Thus, these two perspectives present different assumptions on the sequence of political-socialization, yet each one seems to be valid for particular type of orientations learned and acquired by the socializee in his life-cycle. For instance, pre-adult political learning relating to the socializee's identification to, and attachment with his basic political unit such as the community, tribe, or Nation remains with him, most probably, for ever; and it seems to be highly resistant to change during his life-time. However, pre-adult political learning of the socializee remains incomplete, and most of it becomes changed in conformity with recent experiences obtained by him during adulthood. His greater cognitive maturity that usually accompanies his biological maturity; his observation of the political process and participation in it; his educational attainment; and also his geographic and social mobilities entail for him new socialization experiences which may significantly change, modify, and correct his pre-adult political learning.

Therefore, political learning of the individual from childhood to adulthood seems to be a gradual one that proceeds from the learning of basic political identifications to specific political issues and policies. Of course, political socialization is a complex process, and for explaining its sequence, 'no universally accepted answer exists'.[54]

6.5 Inference

On the whole, "Political-Socialization", as the process of political learning, involves enquiry and analysis of "(a) who, (b) learns what, (c) with what effects".[55] In this process, the individual is the learner, and he tends to learn explicitly political orientations as well as politically relevant non-political orientations as a consequence of his exposure to, and interactions with the socializers or agents of political-socialization. However, as a political-socializee, he does not act as a passive recipient of orientations transmitted by the socializers but he tends to be active in seeking and selecting, and in internalizing these transmission and communications.[56] Since the socializers are numerous, and they transmit information in myriad ways, the process of political learning becomes complex and complicated for the socializee. Moreover, his political learning tends to be crucially influenced by a plurality of socio-economic and psychological variables that characterize him. Therefore, in empirical situations, it may be difficult to ascertain accurately those political-socializers which exert paramount influence upon him, and also, to determine precisely the mode and sequence of his political learning.

However, despite all these limitations, the 'political-socialization process' needs to be studied and analyzed as precisely as possible because, through it, the individual's political learning takes place, and his 'political-culture' is formed and shaped by the political socializers. The patterns of 'political-culture' of the people, as formed in the process of 'political-socialization', tend to condition their political behaviour and roles which, in turn, seem to determine significantly the dynamics of the Political System especially with regard to the prospect of its stability or change. In this context, the process of political-socialization, on facilitating the formation of 'homogeneous-allegiant' political-culture in the people, may pave for political stability and viability; on the contrary, there may emerge political instability and demands for vital change or transformation of the Political System, if 'heterogeneous-alienated' political-culture is formed in them through it. Therefore, the "Political-Socialization Process" seems to be a crucial determinant of the dynamics of the Political System, and hence, it deserves scholarly attention and in depth research.

REFERENCES

1. Irvin L. Child, 'Socialization' in G. Lindzey (ed), *Handbook of Social Psychology*. (Cambridge, Mass: Addison-Wesley, 1954), Vol. 2, p. 655.
2. Robert E. Dowse and John A. Hughes, *Political Sociology*, (London: John Wiley & Sons, Reprinted in 1975) pp. 180-182. Originally published by the same Publisher in 1972.
3. Herbert H. Hyman, *Political Socialization: A Study in the Psychology of Political Behaviour*. (New York: The Free Press, 1959).
4. Fred I. Greenstein, 'Political Socialization' in David L. Sills (ed) *International Encyclopedia of the Social Sciences*. (New York: Crow Well-Collier, 1965), Vol. 14, p. 551.
5. Richard E. Dawson and Kenneth Prewitt., *Political Socialization*. (Boston: Little Brown & Co., 1969), p. 13.
6. *Ibid.*, p. 17.
7. Harry Eckstein, 'A Perspective on Comparative Politics: Past and Present'. In Harry Eckstein and David E. Apter (eds), *Comparative Politics: A Reader*. (New York: The Free Press, 1963), p. 26.
8. Gabriel A. Almond, 'A Functional Approach to Comparative Politics' in Gabriel A. Almond and James S. Coleman (eds), *The Politics of Developing Areas*. (Princeton, NJ: Princeton University Press, Paper-back Edn, 1970), p. 27. Originally published by The Princeton University Press in 1960.
9. *Ibid.*, p. 26.
10. David Easton and Jack Dennis, *Children in the Political System: Origins of Political Legitimacy*. (New York: McGraw Hill, 1969), p. 7.
11. *Ibid.*, p. 4.
12. Gabriel A. Almond, 'A Functional Approach to Comparative Politics'. *Op. cit.*
13. David Easton and Jack Dennis, 'A Political Theory of Political Socialization'. In David Easton and Jack Dennis, *Children in the Political System: Origins of Political Legitimacy. Op. cit.*, pp. 47-69.
14. *Ibid.*, p. 49.
15. *Ibid.*, p. 47.
16. Kenneth P. Langton, *Political Socialization* (New York: Oxford University Press, 2nd Printing, 1972), p. 63.
17. Richard E. Dawson and Kenneth Prewitt., Political Socialization. *Op. cit.*, pp. 63-64.
18. *Ibid.*, p. 73.
19. *Ibid.*, p. 67.
20. B.F. Skinner, *Science and Human Behaviour*. (New York: Macmillan, 1964).

Also, Albert Bandura and Richard W. Walters, *Social Learning and Personality Development* (New York: Holt, Rinehart, and Winston, 1963).

21. James C. Davies, 'The Family's Role in Political Socialization'. *Annals of the American Academy of Political and Social Sciences*, No. 361, 1965, p. 11.
22. Fred. I. Greenstein, *Children and Politics* (New Haven: Yale University Press, 1965), pp. 115-118.
23. Richard E. Dawson and Kenneth Prewitt, *Political Socialization. Op. cit.*, pp. 109-110.
    Also, Robert F. Winch, *Identification and Its Familial Determinants.* (Indianapolis: Bobbs-Merrill, 1962).
24. Fred I. Greenstein, *Personality and Politics.* (Chicago: Markham Publishing Co., 1969). Especially pp. 110-114.
    Also, Robert E. Lane, 'Fathers and Sons: Foundations of Political Beliefs.', *American Sociological Review*, No. 24, August 1959, pp. 502-511.
25. T.W. Adorno, Else Frenkel-Brunswic, Daniel J. Levinson, and R.N. Sandford (eds), *The Authoritarian Personality.* (New York: Harper, 1950), pp. 482-483.
26. Robert E. Lane, *Political Ideology.* (New York: The Free Press, 1962) pp. 400-412.
27. T.W. Adorno, *et al.*, *The Authoritarian Personality. Op. cit.*, pp. 242-262.
28. Richard E. Dawson and Kenneth Prewitt, *Political Socialization. Op. cit.*, p. 115.
29. Robert D. Hess and Judith V. Torney, *The Development of Political Attitudes in Children.* (Chicago: Adline Publishing Co, 1967).
30. Richard E. Dawson and Kenneth Prewitt, *Political Socialization. Op. cit.*, p. 146.
31. *Ibid.*, p. 147. Also
    (i) Gabriel A Almond and Sidney Verba, *The Civic Culture: Political Attitudes and Democracy in Five Nations.* (Princeton, N.J., Princeton University Press, 4th Printing, 1972), pp. 361-363. Originally published by the Princeton University Press, USA in 1963.
    (ii) Edgar Litt, 'Civic Education, Community Norms, and Political Indoctrination.' *American Sociological Review*, No. 28, February 1963, pp. 69-75.
32. Richard E. Dawson and Kenneth Prewitt, Political Socialization. *Op. cit.*, p. 166.
33. *Ibid.*, pp. 165-166.

34. *Ibid.*, pp. 165-166.
35. *Ibid.*, p. 155.
36. *Ibid.*, p. 170.
37. *Ibid.*, p. 167.
38. *Ibid.*, p. 127.
39. Gabriel A. Almond and Sidney Verba, *The Civic Culture. Op. cit.*, p. 191. Also,
    (i) Fred I., Greenstein, 'The Benevolent Leader: Children's Images of Political Authority', *The American Political Science Review*, No. 54, December 1960, pp. 934-943.
    (ii) David Easton and Robert D. Hess, 'The Child's Political World', *Mid-West Journal of Political Science*, No. 6, August 1962, pp. 229-246.
    (iii) David Easton and Jack Dennis, *Children in the Political System*: Origins of Political Legitimacy. (New York: McGraw-Hill, 1969).
40. James S. Coleman, *The Adolescent Society*. (New York: The Free Press, 1961).
    Also, Kenneth P. Langton, Political Socialization. (New York: Oxford University Press, 2nd Printing, 1972), p. 125.
41. Gabriel A. Almond and Sidney Verba, *The Civic Culture. Op. cit.*, p. 192.
42. Kenneth P. Langton, *Political Socialization. Op. cit.* pp. 121-124.
43. Herbert H. Hyman, 'Mass-media and Political Socialization: Role of Patterns of Communication', in Lucian W. Pye (ed), *Communication and Political Development*. (New Delhi: Radha-Krishna Prakashan, Indian Reprint, 1972), p. 129. Originally published in 1963 by the Princeton University Press, Princeton, N.J. (USA).
44. Steven H. Chaffee, L. Scottward, and Leonard P. Tipton, "Mass-Communication and Political Socialization", *Journalism Quarterly*, Vol. 47, 1970, pp. 647-659.
45. Joseph T. Klapper, *The Effects of Mass-Communication* (New York: The Free Press, 1960). pp. 15-16; 45-49.
46. Cecil A. Gibb, "Leadership", in Gardner Lindzey (ed), *Hand Book of Social Psychology*, Ill (Reading, Mass: Addison-Wesley, 1954) pp. 877-917.
47. Richard E. Dawson and Kenneth Prewitt, *Political Socialization, Op. cit.*, pp. 186-191.
48. *Ibid.*, p. 194.
49. *Ibid.*, p. 193.
50. Paul Allen Beck, "Role of Agents in Political Socialization", in S.A. Renshon (ed), *Handbook of Political Socialization: Theory and Research*, (New York: The Free Press, 1977), p. 117.

51. Robert Weissberg, *Political Learning, Political Choice, and Democratic Citizenship*. (Englewood Cliff, N.J.: Prentice-Hall, 1974) pp. 23-31.
52. Richard E. Dawson and Kenneth Prewitt, *Political Socialization, Op. cit.*, p. 43.
53. Dean Jaros, *Political Socialization*. (New York: Praeger, 1973), p. 57.
54. Robert Weissberg, *Political Learning, Political Choice, and Democratic Citizenship. Op. cit.*, p. 30.
55. Fred I. Greenstein, 'Political Socialization', in David L. Sills (ed), *International Encyclopedia of the Social Sciences*, Vol. 14, *Op. cit.*, p. 552.
56. Jack Dennis: 'Major Problems of Political Socialization Research', in Jack Dennis (ed), *Socialization to Politics: A Reader*. (New York: John Wiley and Sons, 1973), p. 21.
    Also, Sandra Kenyan Schwartz and David C. Schwartz, "New Directions in the Study of Political Socialization", in David C. Schwartz and Sandra Kenyan Schwartz (eds), *New Directions in Political Socialization*. (New York: The Free Press, 1975), pp. 6-8.

7

Political Communication

7.1 The Concept

"Political-Communication", in the general sense of the term, connotes the process of communication that occurs in the political context, i.e. in the context of the dynamics of the Political System. It, therefore, involves communication of explicitly political information as well as politically relevant non-political information that tend to enliven the Political System, and influence its dynamics. Of course, definitions and notions on the concept of 'Political-Communication' are many and varied. Hence, the notions and views of some eminent scholars may be noted and analyzed.

Gabriel A. Almond considers 'Political-Communication' as the process of "flow of information from the society to the polity, and in the polity, from political structure to political structure"[1]. He likens the political-communication function to the function of circulation of blood in the body-politic in which demands are transmitted through the veins to the heart, and from the heart through the arteries flow the outputs of rules, regulations and adjudications[2]. It, thus, involves transmission of information both "within the political system, and between the political system and its environment",[3] and consequently, the Political System is enabled to become dynamic and functional. Hence, the 'political-communication function', according to Almond, constitutes "a necessary prerequisite"[4] for performance of other systemic-functions of the Political System for attainment of the goal of 'systemic-maintenance'.

Karl W. Deutsch views 'Political-Communication' as the process of collection of politically relevant information, and their transmission to "the points of decision-making" in a Political System"[5]. It, according to him, influences and controls the performance of the Political System in the context of the latter's survival, growth, and development[6], because political information as transmitted through the process of political-communication may help-form desired habits in the people for rendering habitual obedience to authoritative decisions. Therefore, the Political System, Deutsch believes, tends to function as a "Cybernetic-Apparatus"[7] or a "net-work of communication channels"[8] for generating and fostering supportive attitude and behaviour in the people towards it.

Political Communication, as viewed by David Easton[9], involves transmission of information within the Political System as well as between the Political System and its environment. It facilitates the formation and flow of 'inputs' into the Political System, conversion of 'inputs' into 'outputs', and also flow of the 'outputs' from the Political System into the environment. The Political System, thus, is enabled to work as a self-steering and self-regulating system, and to persist in a situation of either stability or change. According to Easton, the Political System may be said to persist as long as it is able to allocate values for the Society, and to get these allocations accepted as authoritative by most of its people. These two capabilities, what Easton terms as "life-conditions" or essential variables, may be retained by the Political-System, and consequently, it may be enabled to persist through time provided it reduces "stresses" on performing of the function of political-communication through various communication mechanisms and structures, and generates, at the minimum, "diffuse-support" in the people towards it.

Lucian W. Pye[10] considers 'Political-Communication' as the process of communication within the domain of politics. The flow of information in the political-communication process, according to him, determines not only the individual's political behaviour but also the performance of the Political System as well as the direction and pace of socio-political development. 'Political-Communication', for the individual, facilitates his comprehension of the substance of Politics at any particular time, and simultaneously, it is through "the communication process that the host of random actions which represent the pursuit of power by people throughout a society are placed in some form of relationship with each other; that order is established in the sphere of power-considerations, and a society finds that it has a polity."[11] Therefore, the individual's political behaviour, the pattern of political life of the people, the structure and performance of their Political-System, and the level of their political-modernization and development tend to be crucially influenced by the content of political information as transmitted and disseminated in the communication process.

R.R. Fagen defines "Political-Communication" as "communicatory activity considered political by virtue of its consequences, actual and potential, that it has for the functioning of the political system."[12]

Ithiel de Sola Pool[13] opines that 'Political-Communication' involves transmission and dissemination of political-information including signal, symbols, and messages that influence the individual's political behaviour, and also the performance of the Political System.

Dan D. Nimmo and Keith R. Sanders[14], define 'Political-Communication' as a process encompassing all politically relevant communication activities.

R.B. Meadow defines 'Political-Communication' as "any exchange of symbols or messages that, to a significant extent, have been shaped by or have consequences for the functioning of the political systems."[15]

Jean Blondel describes 'Political-Communication' as "the dynamic movement of demands and decisions from one part of the political system to another."[16] He emphasizes on the overriding importance of communication in the life of the political system as he finds that "neither inputs nor outputs can take form, exist, or be related and affect the polity at large without the thread of communication."[17] According to him, "communication links together the parts of the system, and also the present with the past and the future so that demands are followed by policies"[18] and hence, "no operation of the political system can take place unless the parts of the system communicate with each other."[19]

Michael Rush and Philip Althoff consider 'Political-Communication' as "transmission of politically relevant information from one part of the political system to another"[20] and also between the social and the political systems. They point out that political-communication imparts dynamism to the political system as it initiates and influences not only the formation of the individual's political orientations and dispositions but also the performance of other systemic-functions by their corresponding structures.

A review of these notions and definitions reveals that the "Political-Communication Phenomenon" is of tremendous relevance for the dynamics of the Political System. However, its relevance seems to be viewed and comprehended in two different perspectives such as: (i) the 'Homeostatic Perspective'[21] and (ii) the 'Equilibrium Perspective'.[22]

7.2 Homeostatic Perspective

This perspective is pioneered by Karl W. Deutsch who, on being tremendously influenced by the theory of 'Cybernetics', envisions the Political System as a 'Cybernetic Appraratus',[23] and explains its dynamics exclusively in communication terms. The theory of 'Cybernetics', as conceptualized by Norbert Weiner,[24] is a theory of communication and control that comprehends all machines and organizations exclusively as communication systems, and that explains their dynamics on the basis of flow of information. Every system is, thus, viewed as an information-processing apparatus, and its survival, growth, and development tend to be crucially determined by the flow of information from the environment into it, and its ability to react to such information. This 'Cybernetic Theory' is employed by Karl W. Deutsch for analyzing the dynamics of the Political System exclusively in communication perspective.

The analysis of Deutsch is founded on his fundamental assumption that Politics is the process of making decisions on societal goals, and of enforcing them for goal-attainment[25]. Therefore, the prime concerns of Politics are: (i) decision-making on societal goals, and (ii) effective enforcement of these decisions. As the relevance of making decisions and policies on societal goals depends upon their effective enforcement, the core-area of Politics, according to Deutsch, is "the area of enforceable decisions"[26]. Of course, effective implementation of these decisions requires people's obedience and compliance, and hence, Politics involves "the steering or manipulation of human behaviour by a combination of threats of enforcement with habits of compliance."[27] No doubt, threats of force exercised by the 'Political-Authority' or Government may coerce the people to render obedience to the authoritative decisions, but force alone cannot constitute a durable basis of political obedience as 'will' not 'force' is the basis of the State. Therefore, voluntary obedience born out of the free 'will' of the people may facilitate effective implementation[28] of authoritative decisions which, in turn, may pave for attainment of societal goals. As such, Politics is vitally concerned with formation of the 'will' for voluntary compliance and habitual obedience in the people toward the 'political-authority' and the authoritative decisions so that the Society may survive, grow, and develop through time. Therefore, Deutsch postulates that the essence of Politics is "the dependable co-ordination of human efforts and expectations for the attainment of the goals of the society."[29], and that the Political System is the system of "decision and control"[30] designed for attainment of societal goals on securing voluntary compliance of the people for its authoritative decisions.

As survival of the Political System crucially depends upon its ability to secure people's voluntary compliance to its decisions and policies, it tends to function incessantly, and also essentially as a mechanism of communication and social learning[31] for forming and fostering in them the required will and habit of obedience, and for acquiring legitimacy as well. Hence, Deutsch believes that the "inner source of political power" is legitimacy[32], which consists of 'the relatively coherent and stable structure of beliefs, values, memories' for rendering voluntary compliance and habitual obedience to the decisions of the Political System; and that the creation of legitimacy in the people mostly depends upon the facilities for effective socio-political communication both from the past to the present, and between contemporaries.

7.2.1 Cybernetic Analysis

In view of the tremendous relevance of the 'political-communication process' for the over-all performance of the Political System, and of its determining impact upon the latter for survival, growth and development, Deutsch conceptualizes the Political System as essentially a "Cybernetic-Apparatus"[33] or a "net-work of communication channels"[34] that receives and transmits information, in countless ways, for forming supportive orientations, legitimacy, and habitual obedience in the people towards it. Basing on this assumption, he constructs the "Cybernetic Model" of the Political System, and elaborately explains its dynamics. Deutsch's model, in a simplified form, is illustrated in the following diagram.

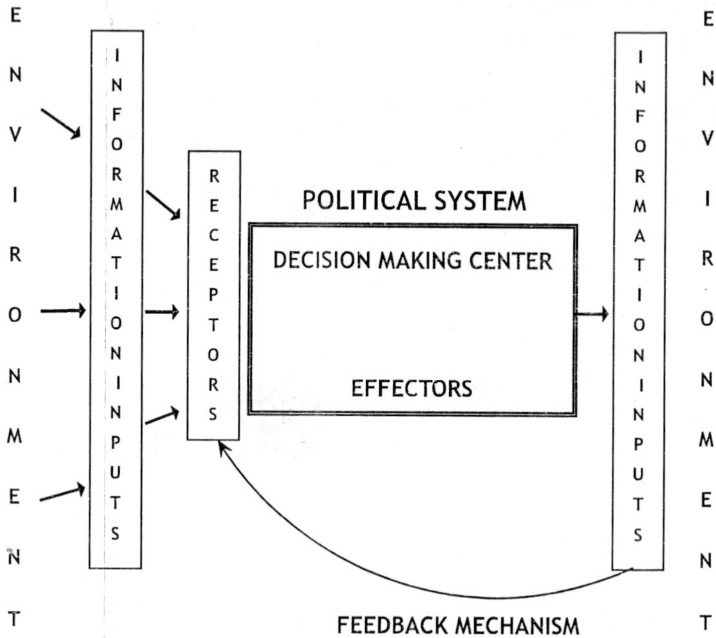

A Simplified Cybernetic Model of the Political System[35]

According to Deutsch, the Political System, as a 'Communication Mechanism', exists in, and also constantly interacts with the environment which is composed of the National Society as well as the International Society. The environment, as a whole, tends to influence the Political System by way of help-forming information-inputs which consist of demands of the people on varieties of societal issues and their support towards the Political System. These information-inputs that are formed as a consequence of the impact of the environment on the people are received initially by some structures such as pressure-groups and political parties which work as 'Receptors' for the incoming 'information-inputs'.

These 'Inputs' that flow from the environment, both domestic and foreign, are, however, not passively received by the 'Receptors', but are subjected to the process of scanning and selection, and then, these are transmitted to the 'decision-making centre' of the Political System. The 'Receptors', thus, work to activate the Political System on feeding it with "inputs of information" which constitute the basis for making of authoritative decisions. Consequently, the Political System is enabled to function as a self-steering apparatus.[36] The self-operation of the Political System commences as and when its 'decision-making centre' responds actively to the 'information-inputs', and produces 'information-outputs'. It performs this self-steering function through structures which may be termed as "Effectors" because these are involved with the performance of the task of processing the incoming information, and giving effect to the 'information-outputs'. In reality, the "Effectors" are the structures such as the legislature, the executive, and the judiciary which also act as communication mechanisms for processing 'information-inputs', and for producing 'information-outputs' in the form of authoritative policies, laws, rules and regulations. The processing of incoming information by the 'Effectors' in the decision-making centre of the Political System involves active scrutiny and selection of these 'information-inputs' which are, therefore, referred to the information stored up as "Memory"[37], and "Values"[38] of the Polity. 'Memory' connotes information on decisions already made by the Government in the past on relevant events and occasions, and stored up in official files, reports, and documents; whereas "Values" connote the political ideals and norms enshrined in the Constitution of the Polity that provides guidelines for making of laws and public policies for attainment of societal goals. Information stored up as 'memory' and information on political 'values' enshrined in the Constitution, together, constitute the referral points for the scrutiny and selection of the 'information-inputs' by the 'Effectors', and for the production of 'information-outputs' by the latter as well.

7.2.2 Servo-Mechanism

Thus, the Political System works as a self-steering 'communication-mechanism' in responding to the incoming environmental information and processing these into 'information-outputs'. However, the survival, and growth of the Political System seem to depend, to a great extent, upon its ability to work as a self-regulatory system[39] by way of responding to the feed-back information about its performance, and of changing its self, if required, on the basis of such information so as to acquire legitimacy of the people. It is, therefore, immensely benefited by the "Feedback mechanism" or "Servo-mechanism"[40] as termed by Deutsch who defines it as "a communications network that produces action in response to an input of information, and includes the results of its own action in the new information by which it modifies its subsequent behaviour".[41] The Political System, thus responds to, and processes feedback information which may be positive or negative[42]. Feedback information, may be said to be positive if it supports and reinforces the original action of the Political System; whereas it may be said to be negative if it opposes the system's original outputs; and it demands for a change in the system's behaviour that will lead closer to the attainment of relevant goals. Therefore, in view of the necessity of the Political System's viability, negative feed-back information seems to be more useful than the positive feed-back information because it makes the Political System aware of its shortcomings and errors, and requires it to regulate or change the 'out-puts' in satisfaction to the demands of the people. Thus, the Political System is enabled by the "Servo-mechanism" to steer itself toward goal-attainment and survival by way of regulating and modifying its original 'out-puts' and policies in conformity with the negative feedback information. Of course, the "Servo-mechanism" may enable the Political System to function as a goal-seeking, goal-changing, and self-developing system provided the latter sincerely responds to, and acts upon the negative feedback information. However, the extent of utility of the feedback information for the Political System, according to Deutsch, tends to be crucially determined by four other major factors such as 'Load', 'Lag', 'Gain', and 'Lead'.[43] 'Load' refers to the volume of negative feedback information transmitted to the 'decision-making centre' of the Political

System. 'Lag' refers to the delay that occurs between the time of availability of feedback information at the 'decision-making centre' and the action taken by the Political System on such reported information. 'Gain' represents the extent of benefit that the Political System is likely to obtain on taking-corrective step, and on moving closer towards goal-attainment. 'Lead' connotes the capability of the Political System to anticipate, and to predict accurately the probable consequences of the negative feedback information, and to undertake corrective steps for survival and goal-attainment. In this context, as Deutsch points out, the prospect of success in goal-attainment is inversely related to the amount of load and lag, and positively related to the amount of gain and lead.[44] These factors such as load, lag, gain and lead, and the pattern of their inter-play tend to determine conjointly the extent of utility of the feedback information for the Political System.

7.2.3 Systemic-Homeostasis

Thus, the Political System functions essentially as an open, self-steering, and self-developing cybernetic-system. However, its dynamics tends to be crucially affected by its combinatorial richness[45] as determined by its ability to perform "Creative intelligence function"[46] by which "information is stored, processed and evaluated."[47] According to Deutsch, the Political System, for becoming self-steering, must receive information from three sources: (i) from its past, (ii) from its external environment (i.e. the totality of the environment composed of the International Society and the National Society in which it exists and operates), and (iii) from its internal environment (i.e. the totality of the elements or structures of which it is composed). All these information must be transmitted to the "Decision-making Centre" of the Political System through various communication-channels. Therefore, the channels of communication through which the Political System receives information ought to be many and varied, and also, these channels must be responsive to the incoming information, and must transmit them with fidelity and accuracy. These information-inputs constitute the basis for making of decisions by the Political System which, while processing them, ought to recall and consult relevant past experiences as stored in the

"Memory" in the form official files and documents. Moreover, the Political System, in order to function as a self-growing and developing system, must respond to the feedback information, evaluate them, and also undertake corrective action as deemed necessary for its survival, growth, and development. Hence, the various channels of communication need be refined so that true, relevant, and adequate information may be transmitted from the environment to the Political System, and also from the Political System to the environment. Simultaneously, the Political System must open up itself to receive and process actively the incoming information; to accord due attention to the feedback information and to evaluate its own performance; to develop its learning capacity and its capacity for innovation and change; and to diversify the range of its goals, and to modify its norms, forms and policies in conformity with people's opinions and demands for obtaining their legitimacy so that it may survive, grow, and develop through time.

Thus, the "Homeostatic perspective" of Karl W. Deutsch portrays the Political System as an open, self-steering, and self-developing 'Communication-mechanism', and explains its over-all dynamics exclusively in communication terms. It is termed as the "Homeostatic perspective" because it envisions the Political System as a change-prone communication system which may change its political values, norms, form or structure, and public policies, if necessary radically and frequently, in conformity with the content of the incoming information from the environment so as to obtain legitimacy of the people on keeping them satisfied, and thereby, to ensure its survival and growth.

7.3 Equilibrium Perspective

This perspective is pioneered by Gabriel A. Almond who explains the relevance of the "Political-Communication Function" for the dynamics of the Political System in the context of the latter's endeavour to maintain its 'structure' and 'culture' intact, and to ensure its stability or equilibrium. According to Almond, the 'political-communication function' is the most basic and fundamental function in the context of the System's dynamics because its performance enlivens the Political System as a whole on initiating the functional process of the latter's constituent structures, and also because its performance may contribute substantially towards attainment of the ultimate goal of systemic-maintenance. As he succinctly points out: "...it is essential in characterizing a political system to analyze the performance of the communication function. Just because of the fact that all the political functions are performed by means of communication, political communication is the crucial boundary-maintenance function".[48] However, despite its tremendous relevance for the dynamics of the Political System, the 'political-communication function' is only one among the latter's several other essential functions. As he emphasizes: "At first thought, it might appear that there is no political communication function as such, that communication is an aspect of all the other political functions. But a view such as this comes into conflict with the fact that in the modern political system differentiated media of communication have arisen which have developed a vocational ethics of neutral or objective communication. This ethics requires that the dissemination of information ought to be separated from the other political functions such as interest articulation, aggregation, and recruitment."[49] He further asserts: "The performance of the communication function does not include all the other political functions, but it constitutes instead a necessary prerequisite for performance of other functions."[52] Thus, Almond proposes that the "functional analysis" of the "political-communication phenomenon" would facilitate meaningful comprehension of its relevance for the dynamics of the Political System.

7.3.1 Functional Analysis

Functional analysis of the "political-communication phenomenon", according to Almond, involves an analysis of the performance of the function of political-communication by various structures, the various styles of its performance, and the implications of its performance upon other systemic-functions.

7.3.1.1 Communication Structures

The structures which perform the function of political-communication,

Almond suggests, may be categorized into five major types such as: (i) Informal Face-to-Face Contacts, (ii) Traditional Social Structures, (iii) Political Output Structures, (iv) Political Input Structures, and (v) Mass-media.[51]

'Informal face-to-face contacts' are informal channels of communication which emerge and operate when a group of individuals interact with one another informally. In these informal group-interactions, a vital role is played by the opinion-leader who, because of his higher social-status or position, is listened to by others with great attention and admiration. The opinion-leader, as the term implies, becomes instrumental in forming opinion of the members of the informal group because he interprets information concerning political and public affairs received through the mass-media or other sources, and transmits these information to his friends, co-workers, or neighbours with whom his interacts regularly and informally.

Traditional Social Structures are organized traditional social groups characterized by formal structure, membership and leadership. Instances of these structures are tribal and caste groups, religious and ethnic groups, etc. that are formed in an organized way mostly in the traditional societies. The primary function of these groups is discussion and deliberation on group-related issues. In these groups, key role is played by the group-leader such as the tribal head in the tribal group, the caste-head in the caste group, or the priest in the religious group. The leaders of these traditional groups, apart from deliberating on group-related issues, also discuss on public and political affairs, and thereby, they help-transmit political and politically relevant information to the members of these respective groups.

'Political Output Structures' are formal governmental structures of the Political System concerned with the making and implementation of the authoritative decisions or outputs. Examples of such structures are the legislature, the executive, and the judiciary; and their primary functions are rule-making, rule-application, and rule-adjudication respectively. However, these output structures also perform the communication function because people are to be informed of the laws, rules and regulations as enacted by the legislature; executive orders as issued and implemented by the executive; and judicial decisions and adjudications as made by the judiciary.

'Political Input Structures' such as pressure-groups, and political parties constitute another category of significant information channels, even though their primary functions are interest-articulation and interest-aggregation respectively. Pressure-groups articulate the demands and interests of their members; and political parties aggregate such articulated interests into alternative policy-proposals in the form of manifestoes which constitute the basis for making of authoritative decisions by the Authority of the Political System. Thus, the input structures are concerned with transmission of demands of the people to the Political System, and as such, they come to play vital roles in the process of political communication.

Mass-media such as Newspaper, Radio, Television, Books and Magazines etc. constitute specialized structures for the performance of political-communication function because their primary function is transmission of information. It is through the 'mass-media' that the people and also all components of the Political System are specifically informed of political as well as politically relevant information.

These communication-structures such as Informal Face-to-Face Contact, Traditional Social Structures, Political Output Structures, Political Input-Structures, and Mass-media are thus involved with transmission of political information. However, efficient and effective performance of the function of political-communication requires that they must have autonomny[52]. An autonomous structure is one which is free of domination and control either by the Government or by particular vested interests in the Society. Enjoyment of autonomy, therefore, enables the communication-structure to transmit information with fidelity, and without distortion.

Of course, among these various communication-structures, there is the prospect of autonomy only for the "Mass-media" as their primary and exclusive function is communication and dissemination of information; whereas for other communication-structures, there is no prospect of autonomy as these are not specifically specialized communication structures, and in reality, are always controlled and dominated either by the vested interests of individuals and groups, or by the Government. Even for mass-media, autonomy is usually denied in the closed and undemocratic Societies where the Government or the vested interest-groups exercise control on them. In these Societies where there is domination or control over the mass-media, the latter cannot perform the function of political-communication with efficiency and effectiveness. Consequently, because of censorship and non-transmission of true, relevant, and adequate information, there may be created an information gap between the people and Government; and hence, the Political System may experience instability for want of support and legitimacy of the people. Therefore, the Political System, in order to remain stable and viable for long on acquiring legitimacy of the people, must provide autonomy to the communication-structures, especially to the specialized "Mass-media", so as to enable them to transmit and disseminate true, relevant, and adequate information, and thereby, to create the right kind of psychological and behavioural environment that would be conducive for political stability and viability. This may be possible, according to Almond, only in the "Democratic Society" as the latter grants and ensures autonomy to the "Mass-media", and allows free-flow of information within the Society and also to it from the extra-societal environment. Therefore, Almond emphatically points out: "Effective political action must be based on rational calculation which, in turn, requires information. A democratic system provides for a relatively free, multi-directional flow of information, thus making it possible for all the structures to calculate and to act effectively."[53]

7.3.1.2 Styles of Communication

These various communication-structures may perform the function of political-communication in varieties of styles. According to Almond, there may be discerned four pairs of style of political-communication such as: (i) Manifest or Latent Style, (ii) Specific or Diffuse Style, (iii) Particular or General Style, and (iv) Affectively-neutral or Affective Style.[54] "Manifest-style" involves transmission of an explicitly political message which is understood by the reader or the audience directly; whereas "Latent-style" involves transmission of non-political information with potential political implications; and the reader or the audience would draw political inferences from these non-political information and expressive cues. "Specific-style" is characterized by transmission of information concerning specific political event; whereas in case of "Diffuse-style", political-information is transmitted in a vague and non-specific way.

In "Particular-style", political-information is transmitted for the consumption of only a distinct or estoteric-audience; whereas "General-style" is characterized by transmission of political-information for the awareness of all components of the Polity and the people of the Society as a whole. "Affectively neutral-style" involves transmission of objective information without any political bias or prejudice; whereas "Affective-style" involves transmission of value-loaded political information. These different styles tend to characterize the modes of transmission political-information by the various communication-structures. However, modern styles of political communication, Almond[55] points out, are the manifest, specific, general, and affectively-neutral styles as distinguished from the latent, diffuse, particular, and affective styles that characterize the communication-structures in transitional and traditional Societies. Moreover, apart from the modern styles of communication, all communication-structures of a modern Polity, according to Almond,[56] tend to transmit homogeneous political-information, and that too with greater mobility and volume; and the flow of information through them tend to become multi-directional. Moreover, these are also expected to transmit true, relevant, and objective political-information, free from biases and prejudices, so that the content of their communications becomes homogeneous. The communication-structures are also required to modernize themselves in respect of equipment and personnel so that greater volume of political-information may be transmitted with greater mobility, and these political information may become available to the people, at large, easily and quickly; and at the same time, the flow of political-information through the communication-structures is required to be multi-directional in the sense that the functions of both input-feeding and output-dissemination may be done by them easily and efficiently.

Thus, the communication-structures perform the function of political communication in varieties of styles and ways, and they become instrumental in making the Political System dynamic and functional on help-forming 'Inputs' and 'Outputs'. Therefore, the performance of the function of political-communication by the "Communication Structures" may significantly influence the performance of other functions of the Political System.

7.3.1.3 Implications for Other Systemic Functions

According to Almond, there may be discerned, in the dynamics of the Political System, three major functional aspects such as: (i) Conversion functions, (ii) System-maintenance and adaptation functions, and (iii) Systemic-capabilities.[57] The performance of these systemic functions, Almond opines, tends to be significantly influenced by the content of political communications as transmitted by the "Communication Structures".

Conversion functions[58] are concerned with the conversion of "Inputs" into "Outputs", and these are the functions of interest-articulation, interest-aggregation, rule-making, rule-application, and rule-adjudication. Performance of these functions by their corresponding structures requires availability of relevant and true information to them. For performing the function of interest-articulation by the pressure-groups, the latter must be provided with information relating to the demands and interests of their members. These interests and demands of the people on varieties of issues pertaining to them also must be communicated to the political parties in order to enable them to perform the function of interest-aggregation. Political parties, thus, prepare alternative policy-proposals in the form of party-manifestoes which constitute the basis for the formulation and enactment of laws by the legislature. Simultaneously, the implementation of the laws by the executive necessitates that the latter as well as the people and other components of the Political System must be communicated with relevant information. Moreover, the laws and rules made by the legislature, and implemented by the executive may generate grievances in the people and other components of the Political System, and these grievances, on being communicated to the judiciary for redress, would enable the latter to perform the function of rule-adjudication. Thus, these various sub-types of conversion functions may be performed by their corresponding structures with effectiveness and efficiency only when each of them is provided with true, relevant, and adequate political information. In case of distortion of information, or supply of irrelevant or inadequate information, the performance of the conversion functions by the corresponding structures relating to the formation of 'inputs', processing of 'inputs' and their conversion into 'outputs' may be adversely affected, and consequently, the 'outputs' produced by the Political System may become flaw-ridden, irrelevant, or inadequate for realization of societal goals. Such a situation may result in loss or decline of support of the people to the Political System, and culminate in political instability and social disintegration.

The performance of the political communication function by the communication-structures may also cast significant impact on the Political System in the context of performance of its maintenance and adaptation function, what Almond terms as the function of 'political socialization'.[59] As and when the communication-structures transmit and disseminate political and politically relevant information, there ensues the process of political socialization because people learn and acquire political orientations and dispositions as well as politically relevant non-political orientations and personality-traits; and consequently, patterns of political culture are formed in them. Therefore, the communication-structures, on transmitting political information and politically relevant non-political information, also act as political-socializers, and influence significantly the process of political socialization involving formation of patterns of political-culture in the people. However, on being exposed to the information as transmitted by the communication-structures, different patterns of political-culture such as homogeneous or heterogeneous political-culture, and allegiant or alienated political-culture may be formed in the people. These patterns of political-culture tend to influence crucially the over-all performance of the Political System as well as the prospect of its stability or change. In case of formation of homogeneous and allegiant political-culture in the people on being exposed to homogeneous and system-allegiant political information through the communication-structures, the Political System would most likely remain stable and viable, and be enabled to maintain itself in tact. On the contrary, transmission of heterogeneous and system-alienated political information by the 'communication-structures' would help-form fragmented and alienated political culture in the people, and as a consequence, the Political system, on being deprived of the support of the people would, most likely, experience instability and undergo change. Thus, the prospect of stability or instability, and that of maintenance or change of the Political System seem to depend, to a great extent, on the pattern of political-culture as formed in the people on being exposed to the relevant information through the communication-structures.

At the same time, 'Systemic-capability'[60], what Almond defines as 'the over-all performance of the political system as a distinct unit in the environment', tends to be determined by the way the function of political-communication is performed by the various communication-structures. According to Almond, 'systemic-capability' may be discerned into four types such as "extractive capability, regulative capability, distributive capability, and responsive capability."[61] Extractive-capability refers to the ability of the Political System to extract resources from its people in the form of taxes and personnel for discharging it various functions. Regulative-capability connotes its ability to regulate the behaviour of its people for establishing peace and order in the Society. Distributive-capability involves its ability to distribute goods and services at its disposal for the benefit and welfare of the people. Responsive-capability refers to its ability and propensity to respond to people's opinions, and to be responsible to them for all its acts of omissions and commissions. However, these different types of 'systemic-capability' are inter-related; and the Political System's extractive-capability, distributive-capability, and regulative-capability seem to depend greatly upon its responsive-capability. If the Political System possesses a high 'responsive-capability' in the sense of responding to public-opinion and of remaining responsible to the people, the latter would most likely develop a sense belongingness to it. Hence, they would legitimize the Political System, pay taxes and discharge its various functions willingly and sincerely, and also they would voluntarily obey its laws and decisions. Consequently, the Political System would have high extractive-capability which, in turn, would enable it to have high distributive-capability, and also it would have high regulative-capability. Therefore, the 'responsive-capability' seems to be the vital determinant of other capabilities of the Political System. However, the Political System may have higher responsive-capability provided it functions as an open-system, and allows adequate autonomy to the communication-structures for transmitting true, adequate, and relevant information from the environment to the Political System, and also within the Political System itself.

7.3.1.4 Systemic-Equilibrium

Thus, the dynamics and the over-all capability of the Political System resulting from the performance of the conversion functions and the system-maintenance and adaptation functions tend to be crucially determined by the content of information as transmitted through the 'political communication-structures', and also by their styles of communication. Hence, Almond considers the political-communication function as the most fundamental function of the Political System because its performance by the communication-structures can hinder or enhance the performance of other kinds of systemic-functions, and also the prospect of attainment of the ultimate goal of "systemic-maintenance". By way of performing the communication function, the communication-structures may transmit system-allegiant information, and contribute toward formation of allegiant political culture in the people. On the contrary, communication-structures may transmit system-alienated information that would facilitate formation of alienated political culture in the people. It is the pattern of political culture, whether allegiant or alienated, as formed in the people by the communication-structures that would mostly determine the prospect of attainment of the ultimate goal of systemic-maintenance. Hence, Almond is of the opinion that the political-communication function is required to be performed by the communication-structures in such a way as to help-form the allegiant political culture in the people and thereby, to enable the Political System to maintain itself intact and to retain its equilibrium or *status quo* through time.

7.4 Need for Synthesis

On the relevance of the "Political-Communication Phenomenon" for the dynamics of the Political System, both the 'homeostatic-perspective', and the 'equilibrium-perspective' seem to present realistic conceptualizations, though each one is incomplete in itself alone. In reality, it is found that every Political System strives to maintain equilibrium or stability in respect of its form and norm (i.e. structural arrangement and political-culture), yet no Political System, in reality, is found to remain without political changes. Since, life is dynamic, every Political System, more or less, must change its form and norms in conformity with the changing socio-economic conditions and emerging political ideas and ideologies because rigid resistance to change may entail withdrawal of legitimacy from it, and culminate even in its disintegration or entropy. Therefore, every Political System undertakes endeavours not only to maintain itself intact in respect of the stability of its form and norms but also to bring about changes in them, as deemed necessary, so that it may survive and develop through time. In these endeavours, the 'communication-structures', on performing the function of political-communication, may contribute significantly towards the capability of the Political System to synchronize the need for maintenance, change, and development. Therefore, the 'Political Communication Phenomenon' ought to be viewed in an integrated perspective as contributing to both the 'equilibrium' and the 'homeostasis' of the Political System.

REFERENCES

1. Gabriel A. Almond, 'A Functional Approach to Comparative Politics' in Gabriel A. Almond and James S. Coleman (eds), *The Politics of Developing Areas*. (Princeton, NJ: Princeton University Press, Paperback Edn, 1970), p. 47. Originally published by The Princeton University Press, New Jersey (USA) in 1960.
2. *Ibid.* p. 47.
3. Gabriel A. Almond and G.B. Powell. Jr., *Comparative Politics: A Development Approach*. (New Delhi: Amerind Publishing Company, 2nd Indian Reprint, 1975), p. 29, Originally published by the Little, Brown and Company, Boston (USA) in 1966.
4. *Ibid.* p. 166.
5. Karl W. Deutsch, *The Nerves of Government: Models of Political Communication and Control*. (New York: The Free Press, 1963), p. 161.
6. *Ibid.*, pp. 248-249.
7. *Ibid.*, p. 77 and 145.
8. *Ibid.* p. 150.
9. David Easton, *A Framework for Political Analysis*. (Englewood Cliffs, N.J.: Prentice-Hall, 1965) p. 111.
   ——, *A System Analysis of Political Life*. (New York: John Wiley and Sons, 1965), pp. 29-33, 117-127 and 411-429.
10. Lucian W. Pye., 'Introduction', in Lucian W. Pye (ed.),

Communications and Political Development (New Delhi: Radha Krishna Prakashan, Indian Reprint, 1972), pp. 6. 4-6. (Originally published by the Princeton University Press, Princeton, N.J.: USA in 1963).

11. *Ibid.*, p. 6.
12. R.R. Fagen, *Politics and Communication* (Boston: Little, Brown and Co, 1966), p. 20.
13. Ithiel de Sola Pool, 'Political Communication: Introduction' in David L. Sills (ed), *International Encyclopedia of the Social Sciences*. (New York: Macmillan Company and the Free Press, 1968) volume 3, pp. 90-95.
14. Dan D. Nimmo and Keith R. Sanders, 'Introduction: The Emergence of Political Communication as a Field' in Dan D. Nimmo and Keith R. Sanders (eds), *Handbook of Political Communication* (Beverly Hills, California: Sage Publications, 1981), p. 27.
15. R.B. Meadow, *Politics as Communication*. (Norwood, N.J.: Ablex Publishing Company, 1960), p. 4.
16. Jeam Blondel, *An Introduction to Comparative Government* (London: Weidenfeld and Nicholson, 1969), p. 223.
17. *Ibid.*
18. *Ibid.*
19. *Ibid.*
20. Michael Rush and Philip Althoff, *An Introduction to Political Sociology*, (London: Thomas Nelson and Sons, 1971), p. 160.
21. Karl W. Deutsch, *The Nerves of Government: Models of Political Communication and Control*. *Op. cit.*, p. 161.
22. Gabriel A. Almond, 'A Functional Approach to Comparative Politics' in Gabriel A. Almond and James S. Coleman (eds), *The Politics of Developing Areas*. *Op. cit.*, p. 46.
23. Karl W. Deutsch, *The Nerves of Government: Models of Political Communication and Control*. *Op. cit.*, pp. 77 and 145.
24. Norbert Weiner, *Cybernetics: Or Control and Communications in the Animal and the Machine* (NewYork: Wiley, 1948), p. 19.
    ——, *The Human Use of Human Beings: Cybernetics and Society*. (Boston: Houghton Mifflin, 1950).
25. Karl W. Deutsch, *The Nerves of Government: Models of Political Communication and Control*. *Op. cit.*, p. 118 and p. 254.
26. *Ibid.* p. 254.
27. *Ibid.* p. 242.
28. *Ibid.* pp. 152 and 254.
29. *Ibid.* p. 124.
30. *Ibid.* p. 145.

31. *Ibid.* pp. 52 and 254.
32. *Ibid.* p. 152.
33. *Ibid.* pp. 77-79.
34. *Ibid.* p. 150.
35. *Ibid.* p. 258, *This Diagram is re-draw diagram following Deutsch's detailed presentation of Cybernetic Model of the Political System.*
36. *Ibid.* pp. 27 and 102.
37. *Ibid.* p. 206.
38. *Ibid.* pp. 118 and 210.
39. *Ibid.* pp. 80 and 81.
40. *Ibid.* p. 88.
41. *Ibid.* p. 88.
42. *Ibid.* p. 192.
43. *Ibid.* pp. 187-188.
44. *Ibid.* pp. 188-189.
45. *Ibid.* p. 164.
46. *Ibid.* p. 164.
47. *Ibid.* p. 164.
48. Gabriel A. Almond, 'A Functional Approach to Comparative Politics' in Gabriel A. Almond and James S. Coleman (eds), *The Politics of Developing Areas. Op. cit.*, p. 46.
49. *Ibid.* pp. 45-46.
50. Gabriel A. Almond and G.B. Powell. Jr., *Comparative Politics: A Development Approach. Op. cit.* pp. 165-166.
51. *Ibid.* p. 167.
52. *Ibid.* p. 170.
53. Gabriel A. Almond, "Functional Approach to Comparative Politics" in Gabriel A. Almond and James S. Coleman (eds), *The Politics of Developing Areas, Op. cit.*, p. 48.
54. *Ibid.* p. 49.
55. *Ibid.* pp. 49-50.
56. *Ibid.* p. 50.
57. Gabriel A. Almond and G.B. Powell. Jr., *Comparative Politics: A Development Approach. Op. cit.*, pp. 27-30.
58. *Ibid.* p. 29.
59. *Ibid.* p. 30.
60. *Ibid.* p. 20.
61. *Ibid.* p. 29.

8

Political Participation

8.1 The Concept

The term "Political-Participation" connotes participatory activities undertaken by the individuals and the mass of people in the political process of the Society. As the political process encompasses the entire process of "authoritative allocation of values"[1] for the concerned Society, 'political-participation' involves participatory activities undertaken in the process of (i) genesis of "values" or preferences of the people on societal issues as ventilated in the form of demands, and their transmission to the 'Political Authority' for making of authoritative decisions and policies; (ii) allocation or making of decisions on these demands, at the level of the Government or Political Authority, in the form of authoritative decisions; and (iii) effective implementation of these authoritative decisions on securing voluntary compliance of the people. Therefore, as Lester W. Milbrath[2] defines, political-participation involves all those activities by which people relate themselves to the political process of the Society, and by way of performing participatory activities and roles, influence the process of making of public-policies, and simultaneously, contribute towards maintenance of the stability and viability of the Political System on rendering support to it. Similarly, Herbert McClosky also opines that 'political participation' consists of "those voluntary activities by which members of a society share in the selection of rulers, and directly or indirectly in the formulation of public policy."[3] Thus, 'political-participation', in its nature, is characterized by voluntary, active, and system-allegiant participatory activities and roles which people perform freely in the political process, without being coerced or dictated, in order to influence the public policy-making process in favour of their demands, elect their representatives who constitute the Government, and to help-maintain socio-political peace and order on rendering obedience to governmental decisions and policies. In this context, it may be noted that people may relate themselves to their Political System and the political process in a variety of ways, and hence, the scope of 'political participation', indeed, entails a wide variety of political and quasi-political activities[4] such as exposing one-self to various political information and stimuli; listening to, and participating in discussions and debates on public and political affairs; making of demands for enactment of desired public policies; voting at the elections; conducting election campaigns; contesting at the elections; playing roles as members of political 'input-structures' such as pressure-groups and political parties; performing roles as incumbents of political 'output-structures' such as the executive, the legislature, and the judiciary; dissemination of politically relevant information through informal face-to-face contacts, traditional social structures and groups, and through various specialized communication structures such as mass-media; and also performing other related activities in the context of dynamics of the Political System. Thus, the scope of 'political-participation' is, indeed, very vast and wide, and it comprises all those participatory activities undertaken directly or indirectly by the people of the Society in relation to their Political System and the political process. However, all these activities, as the very term 'political-participation' implies, imbues with allegiance towards the Political System[5], and are required to contribute towards its stability and viability. Hence, the 'political participation phenomenon' seems to entail positive implications for the dynamics of the Political System. Of course, the nature and scope of the political participatory activities may vary among the people because every individual tends to relate himself to his Political System in a distinct way. Consequently, basing on the varying degrees of interest in Politics, and allegiance to the Political System, various types or forms of political participatory activities may be undertaken by the people of the Society. However, for the purpose of meaningful analysis, it is imperative to classify these activities into some major types or forms.

8.2 A Typology of Political Participation

Following the conceptualization of Lester W. Milbrath[6], political participatory activities may be classified into three major types or forms such as: (i) Gladiatorial Activities, (ii) Transitional Activities, and (iii) Spectator Activities. These may be arranged in the following hierarchical order:

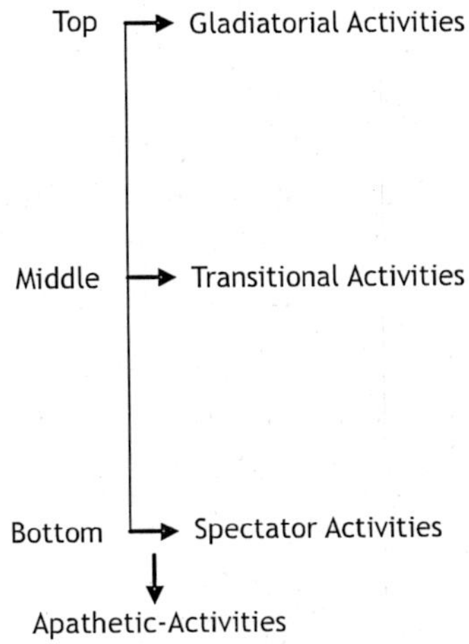

The 'Gladiatorial-activities' are active participatory activities such as holding of public and political offices as Ministers and Members of Parliament; holding of party offices as President and members of the Executive Council, and playing roles in the decision-making process in these offices and institutions; contesting the elections as a candidate and undertaking election campaigns etc. As distinguished from these activities characterized by intense involvement and active participation, the 'Spectator-activities' are characterized by minimal interest and an extremely low level of participation in Politics involving activities such as exposing one-self to political information and stimuli; voting at the elections simply; complying with the directions of the political and party-functionaries etc. Therefore, whereas the 'Gladiatorial-activities' occupy the top position in the hierarchical order of 'political-participation', the 'Spectator-activities' occupy the bottom position. However, in between the top position and the bottom position of the hierarchical order, there may be placed the 'Transitional-activities' characterized by an intermediate level of interest and intensity of participation on performing activities such as attending political and public meetings and rallies; maintaining contact with the political and party leaders; making monetary contribution to the party fund etc. Thus, the transitional-participants tend to be more interested and active than the spectators, but less active and involved in Politics than the gladiators. Of course, this ordering of participatory activities, as Milbrath[7] opines, indicates "a natural progression of being involved in politics", and hence, the participants who are involved at the higher level may also involve themselves at the lower levels. Moreover, those persons who do not undertake any political participatory activity, intentionally or un-intentionally, and hence, stand below the spectators in the hierarchical order of participation may be termed as the 'Apathetics'.[8]

Thus, the 'political-participation phenomenon' compasses varieties of participatory activities of all political-participants including those of the gladiators, the transitional-participants, and the spectators even though wide variations may characterize their activities in respect of the nature, and scope of their participation. These variations in participatory activities seem to originate from various factors such as the psychological needs and social characteristics of the participants, and also the peculiarities of their Political System. Hence, the major factors that tend to determine the pattern of Political participation of an individual need be identified and analyzed.

8.3 Determinants of Political Participation

For discerning the pattern of political-participation of an individual scientifically, it is necessary to enquire into the causal factors or variables, and to find out its inherent 'cause-effect relationship.' Hence, it is imperative to ascertain, in real-world situations, as to why the individual does participate and involve himself in Politics in the way he does. In this context, there may be discerned three major categories of determinants[9] such as: (i) Psychological Determinants, (ii) Social Determinants, and (iii) Political Determinants.

8.3.1 Psychological Determinants

'Political-participation', as Robert E. Lane[10] points out, may stem from the propensity of an individual to fulfil his psychological needs. These needs may be broadly classified, following the conceptualization of Abraham Harold Maslow[11], into five categories such as: (i) physical needs pertaining to the maintenance and sustenance of the physical body; (ii) needs for safety pertaining to bodily protection; (iii) needs for affection; (iv) needs for self-esteem and go-satisfaction; and (v) needs for self-actualization pertaining to the individual's higher self as a human being. The fulfilment of these needs may necessitate acquisition of vital societal values such as wealth, power, status, recognition, prestige, etc. These societal values may be acquired by the individual through political participation, and consequently, his needs may be gratified. However, for analyzing political participatory activities of the individual as caused by motivations for gratification of his needs (material, social, and moral), it seems imperative to enquire into, and discern his personality traits that tend to condition his psychology and pre-dispositions because, as Herbert McClosky rightly opines, psychological needs of the individual stems from his "personality traits (whether primarily constitutional-genetic or primarily learned)".[12] In this context, the individual's personality may be termed as 'democratic personality'[13] if his psychology is characterized by democratic traits such as sociability or an instinct to be associated with fellow human beings and to share values with them; an open-ego or an instinct for inter-personal trust that issues forth in a warm and inclusive attitude toward others; a sense of self-competence and efficacy; and an attitude of relative freedom from anxiety. These democratic traits tend to induce the individual for active participation and involvement in Politics; and it is found valid by number of empirical studies.[14] Hence, it may be hypothesized that persons with democratic personality characterized by sociability, open ego, inter-personal trust, and sense of self-competence are more likely to participate actively in politics, and to play leading roles than persons with non-democratic personality. Moreover, as research evidences[15] indicate, persons with democratic personality tend to participate actively in Politics for fulfilment of higher level psychic needs such as needs for self-actualization that emanate from a sense of civic obligation and humanness.

Thus, the individual's personality seems to condition his needs, and to induce him to fix the priority among his material needs, social needs, and moral needs for attainment through political-participation. He may participate in Politics for obtaining wealth, power, status and other material objects. He may also participate in Politics for fulfilment of his social needs and for overcoming his loneliness; and as Robert E. Lane points out: "Politics may offer to the lonely-man new opportunities for association with others—the excuse may be politics, the need may be fear of isolation."[16] Moreover, his very social life may create tensions or pain for him, and he may seek to diffuse or reduce these tensions through political participatory activities. Apart from undertaking political participatory activities for fulfilment of material or social needs, he may get himself involved in Politics for realization of his moral needs that include self-actualization needs pertaining to his moral self and also intellectual needs pertaining to his curiosity to know and understand the socio-political process. Thus, 'political-participation' may be accorded an instrumental value by the individual, and he may use it to fulfil his various needs that stem from his psychology and personality. Of course, as these psychological variables are many and varied, and that too with different relative weight, it seems to be a complex and difficult task to ascertain accurately the extent of their impact as motivators and determinants of political-participation.

8.3.2 Social Determinants

The pattern of 'political-participation' of the individual seems to be determined significantly by his "Social Position" in which he finds himself placed in the continua of various social variables. Their crucial roles as determinants of 'political-participation' are emphatically focused by Lester W. Milbrath when he opines that social-position variables "do form personalities, beliefs, and attitudes which, in turns, do cause.....participation in politcs."[17] Of course, these social variables that determine the social-position of the individual, and that cause political participation are many and varied; yet there may be discerned some major social variables such as age, gender, race and ethnicity, income and class, occupation, education, and residence etc. that tend to influence, to a great extent, the participatory activities and roles of the individual in the political process.

8.3.2.1 Age

The importance of 'Age' as a crucial determinant derives from the fact that Politics is considered as the domain of the adults, probably, because of the positive correlationship between biological maturity and cognitive maturity of the individual.[18] In the political process, only on attaining adulthood, the individual is allowed to exercise franchise in the elections, and also to hold responsible positions in political and public institutions. As such, he gets opportunity to play effective political roles only during adulthood. Even during adulthood of the individual, there may be noted different patterns of political-participation. During the 'young' adulthood, he tends to be preoccupied mostly with the problem of searching for job or occupation, getting married and forming a family; and during 'old' adulthood, has tends to be increasingly preoccupied with the problem of retirement from job or occupation, physical illness and inabilities, and also other-worldly considerations. Therefore, the middle-aged adult is likely to be more active and involved in Politics than the young-adult, and the old-adult.[19]

8.3.2.2 Gender

'Gender' or sex of the individual tends to determine the pattern of his political-participation as the Society is male-dominated; and Politics is usually considered as the domain of the males. In pursuance of this societal tradition and belief, parents tend to socialize their children intentionally in gender-relevant orientations and accordingly, divergent patterns of psychology and personality traits are formed in the male and female children. In this process of socialization, parents usually instruct the male-child and the female-child to perform sex-appropriate roles[20]; and they require the male-child to be most active in his interactions with others, and to play leadership roles; whereas they require the female-child to keep herself in-doors, to help the mother in the kitchen, to be submissive, and to be least interested in public affairs. These divergent gender-orientations transmitted deliberately by the parents in the family's socialization process seem to help-form the psychology and personality-traits of the male-child and the female child in different forms; and consequently, the male-child tends to be more active and participant than the female-child in social life. As they grow up and become adults, they carry with them the attitudes and propensities learned in the process of family's socialization, and tend to extend these to the political arena when they play political roles. Therefore, in the sphere of Politics, males tend to be more informed, interested, active and efficacious than females.[21]

8.3.2.3 Income and Occupation

'Income' refers to the amount of money earned by the individual for his livelihood. It enables him not only to satisfy the material needs of life but also to live a life of comforts and leisure free from material worries and anxieties. Simultaneously, it accords him a distinct status in the Society in relation to his fellow human beings. Of course, the economic status of the individual seems to be correlated with his occupation because income is earned through occupation. The individual, for earning his livelihood, engage himself in different types of occupations such as agriculture, business, and profession. However, these occupations not only enable him to earn income for his livelihood but also tend to form his socio-economic status which, in turn, seems to determine the pattern of his political participation. Hence, it may be hypothesized that the higher is the level of his socio-economic status or class as determined by his income and occupation, the greater he may be active and involved in Politics.[22]

8.3.2.4 Education

Education broadens the mental horizon of the individual, develops his cognitive capacities, forms in him a sense of efficacy, and also generates in him the curiosity to understand the total environment including the socio-political process. As such, it makes him psychologically attentive, active, and participant; and simultaneously, it accords him a distinct social status. Therefore, the educated individual tends to be informed, active, and efficacious in the socio-political process. Hence, it may be hypothesized that the higher is the level of education of the individual, the greater may be his interest and participation in Politics.[23]

8.3.2.5 Ethnicity and Caste

Ethnicity and Caste are primordial identities that accord social status to the individual in a traditional society; and hence, these may serve as important social determinants of his participatory activities in Politics.[24] It may, therefore, be hypothesized that the higher is the ethnicity or caste of the individual, the greater may be his participation in Politics. Of course, as the traditional society gradually modernizes itself, the social importance of ethnicity and caste tend to decline, but their political importance seems to have increased in the contemporary Societies as these are politically mobilized and used for obtaining political gains and pay-offs.

8.3.2.6 Residence

Residence or fixity of abode may also serve as a social variable in influencing the political participatory activities of the individual.[25] He may have his residence either in the urban area or the rural area; and it is his dwelling place that may help-form his social status. In this context, it may be noted that an urban-dweller, as compared to a rural-dweller, may have a higher socio-economic status because of greater opportunities for him for higher education, media exposure and information, professional occupation, and greater income. Hence, it may be hypothesized that the frequency and intensity of political participation may be greater for an urban-dweller than a rural-dweller because of his higher socio-economic status, and his residence near the centre of the Society.

Thus, various social variables, traits, and identities, seem to determine conjointly the individual's "Socio-Economic Status (SES)" which, in turn, tend to influence significantly the pattern of his political-participation. In this context, it may be hypothesized, on the whole, that the higher is the socio-economic status of the individual, the greater may be his involvement and participation in Politics.

8.3.3 Political Determinants

'Political-participation' of the individual seems to be influenced by varieties of political determinants among which there may be discerned and analyzed some major factors or variables such as the Political System, Political Parties and Party System, Pressure-Groups, National and International Issues and Crises, and the Individual's Sense of Political Efficacy.[26]

8.3.3.1 The Political System

The 'structure' of the Political System through which authoritative decisions and policies are made and implemented may be classified into two major types such as: (i) the open and democratic Structure, and (ii) the closed and authoritarian structure in terms of location and interplay of legitimate power within it. It is the structure of the Political System, whether it is open-democratic in structure or closed-authoritarian in structure, that tends to determine the pattern of political participation of the people.[27] In the open-democratic Political System, legitimate power flows from the people to the Government which, as a consequence, becomes responsible and responsive to the former; whereas, in the closed-authoritarian Political System, legitimate power remains centred in the Government which imposes its decisions upon the people without being responsible and responsive to them. Therefore, the open-democratic Political System, as distinguished from the closed-authoritarian Political System, provides scope for free flow of political information, and also for freedom of expression of demands, freedom for political assembly and association, freedom for exercising franchise, and freedom for contesting elections and holding political offices. Hence, the open-democratic Political System, on providing motivations and structural opportunities to the people for effective and meaningful political participation, tends to influence the nature and scope of their political participatory activities.

Moreover, 'political-participation' of the individual seems to be influenced by the rules of political game[28] that provide parameters and guidelines for the working of the Political System. These rules are codified as the "Constitutional Provisions" that seek to regulate and control not only the political decision-making process but also the activities and role of all political actors including the ordinary citizens and the incumbents of various political and public institutions. However, the provisions of the Constitution, and the laws and rules of the political game seem to facilitate active political participation and involvement of the people provided these are simple and easily comprehensible to the people at large; whereas complicated and incomprehensible constitutional provisions and rules tend to affect adversely the nature and scope of political participation of the citizens.

8.3.3.2 Political Parties and the Party System

'Political parties' are the inevitable agencies for formation of Government in the democratic Polity. They compete with one another in the electoral battle for obtaining people's mandate for forming the Government. However, for political and electoral competition to take-place, there must emerge in the Society either the multi-party system or, at the minimum, the bi-party system. Moreover, for becoming successful in these political and electoral competitions, political parties seek to obtain support and allegiance of the people, and for this purpose, they organize public meetings, distribute leaflets and manifestoes, conduct political campaigns, and undertake political education of the people through various measures and methods. All these activities of the political parties, and their inter-party competitions not only provide political information to the people but also help-create political interest in them for active and effective political participation.[29]

8.3.3.3 Pressure-Groups

'Pressure-groups' are non-political social groups that represent homogeneous interests of particular groups of population, and seek to exert pressure upon the Government for protecting and promoting their articulated objectives. Even though each of these is characterized by non-political objective, each one performs quasi-political activities, and hence, it may serve as a vital political determinant in influencing the pattern of political participation of its members.[30] These groups tend to make their members active in devising channels of access to the decision-making centre in the Government, and in exerting influence upon the political decision-makers for realizing their objectives. As such, the activities of the pressure-groups seem to create a congenial mind-set for their respective members for active participation and involvement in Politics.

8.3.3.4 Issues and Crises

Awareness of the individual on emerging 'National and International Issues and Crises' may determine the pattern of his political participation'.[31] As and when he becomes aware of pressing national issues such as issues of human rights, civil liberty, social justice, liberalization or nationalization of economy, educational and health-care facilities etc.; and international issues such as nuclear non-proliferation, world-trade, regional co-operation, cross-border terrorism, etc., these may heighten his political interest which, in turn, may motivate him to seek redress through political-participation.

8.3.3.5 Sense of Political Efficacy

The 'sense of political-efficacy' or competence refers to the belief and confidence of the individual in himself that he can influence the Government and the policy-making process successfully. Accordingly, he may work through various institutional means and channels such as political parties, pressure-groups, and mass-media including television, radio, newspapers, journals etc.; and he may even work individually on petitioning the Government, and filing public interest litigation case in the judiciary. While undertaking these peaceful activities in protest against public policies, laws, rules and regulation that he consider unjust, and against which he demands for remedies or amendments, he remains unconcerned as to the extent of actual success in goal-attainment. It is this subjective sense of political efficacy or competence which, however, motivates him for active political participation. Therefore, the pattern of political participation of the individual seems to be greatly correlated to his subjective sense of political-efficacy.[32]

8.3.4 Conjoint Impact of the Determinants

Thus, there may be discerned varieties of psychological, social, and political variables and correlates of political participation. However, these determinants do not function in isolation to one another but tend to determine conjointly the pattern of political participation of the individual. Of course, as the determinants are so many and varied with different relative weight; and as the corelationships between them and the individual's participatory activities are so complex and intricate, it seems to be an arduous task to identify them exactly, and to measure the extent of their impact accurately. Hence, rigorous research endeavours are required for ascertaining them in empirical situations.

8.4 Political Participation and the Political System

"Political-participation" infuses dynamism into the Political System, and enlivens it. As and when the people of a Society perform political participatory roles in the context of formation of 'Inputs' (demands and support), and 'Outputs' (authoritative decisions), and render allegiance to it, the Political System having been endowed with legitimacy becomes a dynamic entity, and functions with stability and viability. Therefore, 'allegiant political participation' seems to be the life-force of every Polity irrespective of the fact as to whether it is large or small in size; and authoritarian or democratic in ideology and structure. In the case of an 'Authoritarian Polity' where freedom for political participation does not exist, and the scope of political participation become extremely limited and directed, the 'Ruler' (or the Government) even invariably tries to clothe his arbitrary decisions with the veil of a mass-approval secured through some form of 'political-participation' of its people. As distinguished from it, the 'Democratic Polity' seeks to secure legitimacy from the people manifestly and directly on providing them opportunities for open, free, and universal political-participation. In this context, Herbert McClosky emphatically points out: "Participation is the principal means by which consent is granted or withdrawn in a democracy, and rulers are made accountable to the ruled."[33] Moreover, free and universal political participation may provide opportunity to the

Government to be benefited by the wisdom and experiences of the people in the matter of policy-making and governance. Simultaneously, it may help-check the self-aggrandizing and unscrupulous tendencies of the Government, and may make the latter responsive and responsible to the people. Hence, in a democracy, as Herbert McClosky asserts, "participation is power"[34]; and as Gabriel A. Almond and Sidney Verba opine: "citizen competence and participation are at the heart of the definition of democracy"[35].

Thus, on contributing toward legitimacy, stability and viability of the Political System, and making the Government responsible and responsive to the 'governed', "Political-Participation" seems to facilitate the process of political development. Scope and opportunity for free and universal political-participation may create and foster in the people a sense of loyalty and belongingness towards the Political System, and hence, may contribute toward formation as well as reinforcement of their national identity which stands out as the first prerequisite of political development. Therefore, as regard the over-all relevance of "Political-Participation" for the Political System, Lucian W. Pye emphatically points out: "Political Development does entail some degree of extended participation.......... participation has a role to play in nation-building activities since it represents a means of creating loyalties and a new feeling of national identity".[36]

REFERENCES

1. David Easton, *The Political System—An Enquiry into the State of Political Science*. (Calcutta: Scientific Book Company, Second Indian Edition, 1971) p. 129. Originally published by Alfred A. Knopf Company, New York in 1953.
2. Lester W. Milbrath and M.L. Goel, *Political Participation* (Chicago: Rand McNally Publishing Co., Second edition, 1977), p. 2.
3. Herbert McClosky, 'Political Participation' in David L. Sills (ed.), *International Encyclopedia of the Social Sciences*. (New York: Collier-Macmillion, 1968), Vol. 12, p. 252.
4. *Ibid*. p. 252.
   Also, Lester W. Milbrath and M.L. Goel, *Political Participation*, *Op. cit.*, pp. 8-11.
5. Herbert McClosky, "Political Participation" *Op. cit.*, p. 252.

6. Lester W. Milbrath, *Political Participation. Op. cit.* p. 18.
7. *Ibid.*, p. 19.
8. Lester W. Milbrath and M.L. Goel, *Political Participation. Op. cit.*, p. 21.
9. Herbert McClosky, "Political Participation" *Op. cit.*, p. 256.
10. Robert E. Lane, *Political Life-Why People get Involved in Politics.* (New York: Free Press, 1959), pp. 101-111.
11. Abraham H. Maslow, *Motivation and Personality* (New York: Harper, 1954).
12. Herbert McClosky, "Political Participation", *Op. cit.*, p. 258.
13. Harold D. Lasswell, Power and Personality. (New York: 1946), p. 148. ——, *The Political Writings of Harold D. Lasswell* (Glencoe, Illinois, 1951) p. 495.
14. (i) Lester W. Milbrath and Walter Klein, 'Personality Correlates of Political Participation', *Acta Sociologica 6* (fasc. 1-2), 1962, pp. 53-66.
    (ii) Robert E. Lane, *Political Life-why People Get Involved in Politics*. (Glencoe, Illinois: Free Press, 1959).
    (iii) James C. Davies, *Human Nature in Politics*. (New York: Wiley, 1963), pp. 34-36.
    (iv) Yasumasa Kuroda, 'Sociability and Political Involvement', *Midwest Journal of Political Science*, 9 (1965), pp. 133-147.
    (v) Pearl Mayo Gore and Julian B. Rotter, 'A Personality Correlate of Social Action', *Journal of Personality*, 341 (1963), pp. 58-64.
    (vi) Roderick Bell, 'The Determinants of Psychological Involvement in Politics—A Causal Analysis', *Midwest Journal of Political Science*, 13 (1969), pp. 237-253.
    (vii) Fred, I. Greenstein, *Personality and Politics—Problems of Evidence, Inference, and Conceptualization*. (Chicago: Markham, Publishing Co., 1969).
    (viii) Sheldon G. Levy, 'The Psychology of Political Activity', *Annals of Political Science*, 391 (1970), pp. 83-96.
    (ix) Fred, I. Greenstein and Michael Lerner (eds), *A Source Book for the Study of Personality and Politics*. (Chicago: Markham, Publishing Co., 1971).
    (x) Jeane Nickel Knutson, *The Human Basis of the Polity—A Psychological Study of Political Man*. (Chicago: Aldine-Atherton, 1972).
    (xi) Stanley Allen Renshon, *Psychological Needs and Political Behaviour—A Theory of Personality and Political Efficacy*. (New York: Free Press, 1974).
    (xii) Paul M. Sniderman, *Personality and Democratic Politics*. (Berkeley: University of California Press, 1975).

15. (i) Angus Campbell, Gerald Gurin, and Warren E. Miller, *The Voter Decides*. (Evanston, Illinois: Row, Peterson, 1954).
    (ii) Angus Campbell, Philip E. Converse, Warren Miller, and Donald Stokes, *The American Voter*. (New York: Wiley, 1960).
    (iii) Christian Bay, 'Needs, Wants, and Political Legitimacy', *Canadian Journal of Political Science*; 1 (1968), pp. 241-260.
    (iv) Robert E. Lane, *Political Thinking and Consciousness—The Private Life of the Political Mind*, (Chicago: Markhan, Publishing Co., 1969).
    (v) Jeanne Nickel Knutson, *The Human Basis of the Polity—A Psychological Study of Political Men*. (Chicago: Aldine-Atherton, 1972).
16. Robert E. Lane, *Political Life—Why People Get Involved in Politics*. (Glencoe, Illinois: The Free Press, 1961), p. 108.
17. Lester W. Milbrath and M.L. Goel, *Political Participation—How and Why do People Get Involved in Politics*, *Op. cit.*, p. 86.
18. Lawrence G. Kohlberg, 'Stage and Sequence—The Cognitive Development Approach to Socialization' in David Goslin (ed), *Handbook of Socialization: Theory and Research*. (Chicago: Rand McNally & Co., 1969) pp. 347-380.
19. (i) N.E. Cutler, 'Aging and Generations in Politics', in A.R. Wilcox (ed), *Public Opinion and Political Attitudes: A Reader* (New York: Wiley, 1974).
    (ii) Robert E. Lane, *Political Life—Why People Get Involved in Politics*. (Glencoe, Illinois: The Free Press, 1959).
    (iii) S.M. Lipset, *Political Man—Social Bases of Politics*. (New York, Garden City: Double Day, 1960).
    (iv) Sidney Verba and Norman H. Nie, *Participation in America: Political Democracy and Social Equality*. (New York: Harper & Row, 1972).
    (v) M.L. Goel, *Political Participation in a Developing Nation: India* (New York: Asia Publishing House, 1975).
20. (i) Fred I. Greenstein, *Children and Politics*. (New Haven: Yale University Press, 1965), pp. 115-118.
    (ii) Robert E. Dowse and John A. Hughes, 'Girls, Boys, and Politics', *British Journal of Sociology*, 22 (March, 1971), pp. 53-67.
21. (i) Gabriel A. Almond and Sidney Verba, *The Civic Culture: Political Attitudes and Democracy in Five Nations* (Princeton, N.J.: Princeton University Press, 1963).
    (ii) Lester W. Milbrath and M.L. Goel, *Political Participation*. *Op. cit.*, p. 116.
22. (i) Robert A. Dahl, *Who Governs?: Democracy and Power in an American City*. (New Haven: Yale University Press, 1961).

(ii) Norman H. Nie, G.B. Powell, Jr. and Kenneth Prewitt., 'Social Structure and Political Participation: Developmental Relationships', Part-I and II, *American Political Science Review*, 63 (1969), pp. 361-378 and 808-832.

(iii) Sidney Verba and Norman H. Nie, *Participation in America: Political Democracy and Social Equality*. (New York: Harper & Row, 1972).

23. (i) Gabriel A. Almond and Sidney Verba, *The Civic Culture: Political Attitudes and Democracy in Five Nations* (Princeton, N.J.: Princeton University Press, 1963) especially, Chapters 3, 4, 7, 9, 10 and 11.

    (ii) Sidney Verba and Norman H. Nie, *Participation in America: Political Democracy and Social Equality*. (New York: Harper & Row, 1972).

24. (i) Angus Campbell, Gerald Gurin, and Warren E. Miller, *The Voter Decides*. (Evanston, Illinois: Row, Peterson, 1954).

    (ii) Sidney Verba and Norman H. Nie, *Participation in America: Political Democracy and Social Equality*. (New York: Harper & Row, 1972).

25. (i) Stein Rokkan and Angus Campbell, 'Norway and United States of America' in Citizen Participation in Political Life, *International Social Science Journal*, 12 (1960), pp. 69-99.

    (ii) William N. McPhee and William A. Glaser (eds), *Public Opinion and Congressional Elections*. (New York: The Free Press of Glencoe, 1962).

26. Herbert McClosky, "Political Participation" *Op. cit.*, pp. 259-262.

27. Lester W Milbrath and M.L. Goel, *Political Participation: How and Why do People Get Involved in Politics*, *Op. cit.*, pp. 144-155.

28. Lester W. Milbrath, 'Individuals and the Government' in Herbert Jacob and Kenneth N. Vines (eds), *Politics in the American States: A Comparative Analysis*. (Boston: Little, Brown & Co., 1971), pp. 27-81.

29. (i) Robert E. Agger, Daniel Goldrich, and Bert E. Swanson, *The Rulers and the Ruled*. (New York: Wiley, 1964).

    (ii) Lester W. Milbrath, 'Political Participation in the States' in Herbert Jacob and Kenneth N. Vines (eds), *Comparative State Politics*. (Boston: Little, Brown & Co., 1965).

30. Robert E. Lane, *Political Life: Why People Get Involved in Politics*. (Glencoe, Illinois: The Free Press, 1959).

31. Herbert McClosky, "Political Participation" *Op. cit.*, pp. 261-262.

32. (i) Gabriel A. Almond and Sidney Verba, *The Civic Culture: Political Attitudes and Democracy in Five Nations* (Princeton, N.J.: Princeton University Press, 1963).

(ii) Lester W. Milbrath and M.L. Goel, *Political Participation. Op. cit.*, p. 58.

(iii) Carole Pateman, *Participation and Democratic Theory*. (London: Cambridge University Press, 1970) p. 46.

33. Herbert McClosky, "Political Participation", *Op. cit.*, p. 253.
34. Herbert McClosky, "Political Participation", *Op. cit.*, p. 263.
35. Gabriel A. Almond and Sidney Verba, *The Civic Culture: Political Attitudes and Democracy in Five Nations* (Princeton, N.J.: Princeton University Press, 4th Printing, 1972), p. 230.
36. Lucian W. Pye, *Aspects of Political Development*. (Boston: Little Brown & Co., 1965), pp. 39-40.

9

Political Movement

9.1 The Concept

The term 'Movement' may be literally defined as "the act or the process of setting in motion as contrasted with quiescence, passivity or inactivity."[1] As such, it tends to stir the *status quo* or the prevalent condition of any aspect of societal-life, and serves to bring about desired changes in it. It manifests, as Rudolf Heberle[2] points outs, in the form of "a commotion, a stirring among people, an unrest, a collective attempt to reach a visualized goal, especially a change in certain social institutions." When such a collective endeavour is organized and undertaken by the people as a vehicle of political change, it may be termed as "Political Movement". Hence, the aim of "Political Movement" is 'desired political change', and its target may be any object of the Political System, or even the Political System as a whole. As, in the Political System, there may be discerned three major constituting objects such as the 'Political Community', the 'Regime', and the 'Authority',[3] the target for change may be any one or all of them comprising the entire Political System. In this context, for instance, demands may be made for changing the structure of the 'Political-Community' on partitioning it into independent sovereign units; demands may be made for changing the 'Regime' (the Constitutional Order) partly or wholly; demands may be made for changing governmental policies or the incumbents of 'Authority'; and even demands may be made for bringing about comprehensive change in the Political System including its 'Political Community',

'Regime', and 'Authorities'. Thus, 'political movement' focuses explicitly on the objective of political change, and strives to attain it on controlling the Political System, or acquiring 'State-Power'. It is this distinctively political objective that seems to differentiate it from 'social movement'; and this distinction is focused by scholars in their study and analysis of 'political movement'. For instance, Andre Gunder Frank and Marta Fuentes[4] opine that the objective of social movement is exclusively social transformation including reform and reformation; whereas the objective of political movement is explicitly political change. However, this differentiation between 'Social Movement' and 'Political Movement' seems to be unrealistic and unfounded as Society and Polity, in reality, tend to inter-penetrate and influence each other in the context of their dynamics. As such, the concept of 'de-politicization of the social realm' is a myth, and the difference between social movement and political movement is merely semantic. Therefore, the term 'Political Movement' ought to be defined and comprehended broadly as a movement that contains political implications. As Rudolf Heberle emphatically argues, "...all movements have political implications even if their members do not strive at political power."[5] This broad perspective on political movement is also advocated by scholars such as Paul Wilkinson,[6] and John Wilson[7]. Hence, in view of the reality of the socio-political process, the realm of 'political-movement' should be broadened to include not only those movements which are characterized by explicitly political objectives but also those social movements which, even though cherish non-political objectives, tend to influence or pressurize the Political System for obtaining favourable policy decisions as deemed necessary for attainment of the cherished objective of social transformation and change.

The concept of 'political-movement', of course, necessarily includes three elements such as: (i) Beliefs or Ideals, (ii) Organization or Structure, and (iii) Actions or Behaviour of its Members.[8] Every political movement is characterized by a distinct set of ideals or system of beliefs, what may be termed as its "Ideology". The ideology of the movement specifies the aims and objectives which are cherished and championed by its members, and sought to be attained by them through concerted action; and it may present and demand for a 'radically different socio-political order' or 'reforms' in the prevalent Political

System. However, the ideology of every political movement contains ideas of its adherents on issues and values of liberty, rights, equality and justice; and some political movements may even combine these with their ideas on national unity and independence. The ideology of the movement may be legitimized by its adherents because of their belief in the truth of the constitutive ideas or the charisma of the leader, or because of personal utilitarian interests.[9] Of course, these grounds of legitimacy are found to be combined, in different degrees, in each political movement. It is this common ideology which is cherished and championed by a set of individuals that binds the adherents by ideological nexus, and facilitates the emergence of the movement. For attainment of the ideology or objective, the movement, of course, needs to be organized. In this context, "organization or structure", in general, means that the group of adherents to an ideology must have, more or less, a well-defined boundary that distinguishes between members and non-members; it must have a 'power-structure' consisting of leaders with hierarchy of positions, superior-subordinate roles, and concentration or diffusion of power; and also, it must have means or strategies for attainment of goals for which both leaders and members work together. Thus, 'organization' enables the movement to co-ordinate and regulate the actions and behaviour of its adherents effectively and smoothly for goal-attainment, and to generate, as well, a broader base of support of the people to its cause. In this context, the leaders of the movement act as 'guides' and 'strategy-makers' for the members, and they also act as the movement's 'authorized spokesmen' and 'representatives' in relation to the people, and to the Government as well. No doubt, the leaders plan the strategies of the movement, and provide necessary directions for their implementation, but effective goal-attainment seems to depend crucially upon the extent of commitment of the members of the movement to its goal, and their activism to attain it on performing required activities and behaviour. Thus, on the whole, the three elements such as 'Ideology', 'Organization', and 'Behaviour' that characterize a "Political Movement" tend to determine, conjointly, its nature as well as the prospect of its success in goal-attainment.

9.2 Causal Factors

'Political Movement' may emerge owing to varieties of factors and conditions. However, there may be discerned three major causal factors[10] such as: (i) Structural Factor, (ii) Socio-Psychological Factor, and (iii) Organizational Factor that seem to be mostly responsible for the emergence of "Political Movement".

9.2.1 Structural Factor

The very 'structure' of the Society may generate political movement. In this context, Marx's[11] analysis of the 'social-structure', exclusively in economic terms, provides one of the most important structural causes for the genesis of political movement and revolution. His fundamental postulate is that the 'social-structure' is merely the manifestation of class-relations which are founded upon relations of production as well as ownership of the means or forces of production. Accordingly, the people of the Society become divided into two classes such as the class of the 'Haves' and the class of the 'Have-nots', and there ensues antagonism and conflict between these two classes for protection and promotion of their respective interests. As 'economic-power' paves for 'political-power', the class of the 'Haves' or the 'Capitalists' design and build the 'structure' of the Society for perpetuating its privileged status; whereas the class of the 'Have-nots' or the 'Proletariat' that remains exploited tends to bring about necessary changes in the socio-political edifice for attainment of justice. Thus, Marx asserts that 'the history of all hither to existing societies is the history of class-struggles', and that the class-based societal-structure characterized by class-antagonisms contains within it the seed of revolutionary political movement. Therefore, "Political Movement" emerges when the class of the 'Have-nots' consisting of the exploited peasants, and industrial-workers become organized into a massive socio-political revolutionary movement against the class of the 'Capitalists' for ending class-exploitation, and establishing the "Just" Society.

However, as different from Marx's analysis, the 'social-structure' is viewed by Max Weber[12] not as class-based but as group-based. According to Weber, the structure of Society including its 'authority-pattern' is mostly designed by the status-groups who provide leadership to the people. The status-groups are marked by their distinctive life-styles, and superior social-status manifested in the ownership of a cluster of material resources, such as property or liquid capital, and the monopoly of symbolic resources such as habits of dress, religious beliefs, or codes of honour and esteem. These groups stand hierarchically in the status-ladder; and there may occur competition and conflict among them for acquisition of societal leadership. It is the propensity of a status-group or groups to advance and realize their ideals on establishing the desired pattern of "Political-Authority" or to attain their symbolic interests through collective-action that may pave for the emergence of political movement in the Society.

Thus, the genesis of 'political movement' is traced by Karl Max and Max Weber, the founding fathers of Political Sociology, to the 'societal-structure' though they view and analyze this causal factor in different perspectives.

9.2.2 Socio-Psychological Factor

The emerging pattern of social-psychology of the people of a Society seems to be the most crucial factor responsible for the genesis of political-movement. As and when they perceive prevalence of 'injustice' in socio-political life or 'non-fulfilment' of their cherished ideals and values, they feel dissatisfied and frustrated, and tend to strike at the imputed source of frustration on organizing political movement. It is this subjective sense of people's "relative deprivation" that constitutes the root cause of the genesis of political movement. In this context, the term "Relative Deprivation" may be defined with Ted Robert Gurr[13] as "the tension that develops from a discrepancy between the 'ought' and 'is' of collective value-satisfaction". In socio-political life, the individuals as well as collectivities come to value many things such as wealth, status, power, security, equality, freedom, national self-determination etc. When they cannot achieve these values that they aspire for, they feel dissatisfied, and become psychologically tension-ridden. In this context, 'ought' refers to the conditions or values of socio-political life that they come to believe they are entitled to; and 'is' refers to their perception of the reality or the injustice committed on them. As and when there emerges any discrepancy or gap between the 'ought' and the 'is' of collective value-satisfaction, people tend to form and feel in them a sense of 'relative-deprivation' that, in turn, makes them dissatisfied and frustrated; and simultaneously, tends to motivate them to organize the political movement in order to remove the cause or the source of their deprivation and frustration, and also to realize the ideals and values they aspire for. This socio-psychological theory of "Relative Deprivation" that amply explains the genesis of "Political Movement" is also upheld by a number of eminent scholars. For instance, Daniel Lerner[14], James C. Davies[15], W.G. Runciman,[16] H. Nieberg[17], and Crane Briton[18] are proponents of this theory.

The subjective sense of 'relative deprivation' which seems to be the most potent cause of the genesis of political movement may be discerned, following the formulation of Ted Robert Gurr, into three major types[19] such as: (i) Inspirational Deprivation, (ii) Decremental Deprivation, and (iii) Progressive Deprivation, and their distinguishing attributes are presented in the following diagrams:

Types of Relative-Deprivation

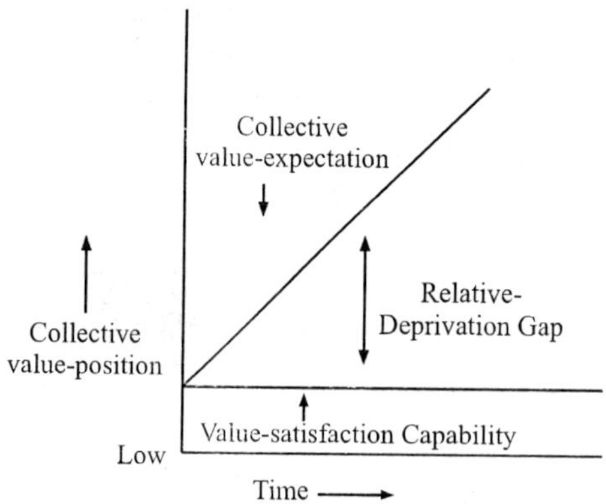

(i) Inspirational Deprivation[20]

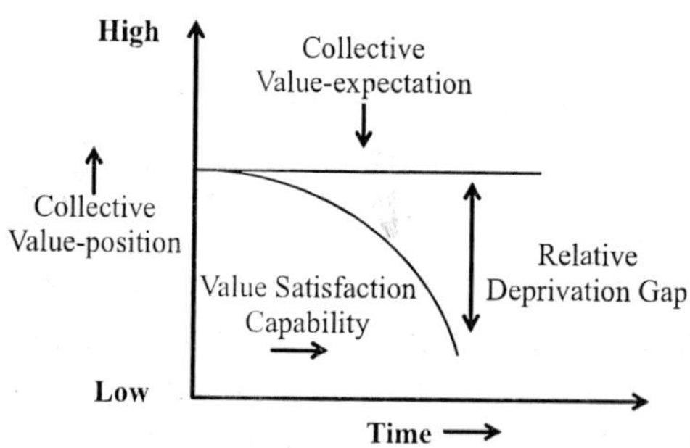

(ii) Decremental Deprivation[21]

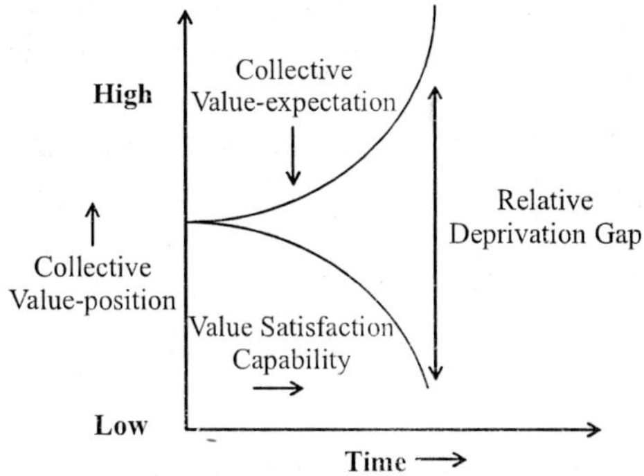

(iii) Progressive Deprivation[22]

"Aspirational-Deprivation" occurs when people's aspirations for desired values rise up high increasingly but the Political System becomes incapable of fulfilling these aspirations, and its capability remains constant. It usually emerges in 'Developing Societies' when the "revolution of rising expectations" of the people for higher living standards produced as a consequence of their exposure to media-communications, and educational attainment remains unresolved by the Political System. Failure to provide congenial conditions for realization of the rising expectations of the people because of incapacity of the Political system generates frustration in the people, and paves for the emergence of political-movement. Moreover, aspirational-deprivation may relate to political values such as rights, liberty, equality, justice, nationalism, Nation Statehood etc., and when the people feel deprived of these aspired political values, there may emerge political movement; as for instance, the aspirations of the people of India for 'National Independence' from the British-rule resulted in the emergence of the independence-movement in 1921 under the leadership of Mahatma Gandhi. As distinguished from 'aspirational-deprivation', the "Decremental-Deprivation" is characterized by the constancy of people's aspirational values, but a decline in the capability of the Political System to fulfil them. In this type of relative-deprivation, people feel frustrated because of loss of values already possessed and enjoyed by them consequent upon a decline in the capacity of the Political System to maintain these values. For instance, if the people of a Society come to perceive that the Authority of their Political System is incapable of maintaining their rights and liberties granted and ensured to them by the Constitution, they may feel frustrated and organize political-movement against it. For instance, such a political-movement had emerged in India in June 1975 when the Government of India under the Prime-Minister 'Mrs. Indira Gandhi' proclaimed 'National Emergency' and grossly flouted the democratic rights and liberties of the people granted to them by the Constitution of India. The third type of relative-deprivation which is termed as "Progressive-Deprivation" may occur when the value-expectations of the people rise up high, and simultaneously, the capability of the Political System to fulfil them sharply declines. Consequently, there occurs an ever-increasing 'relative-deprivation gap' that generates frustration in the people, and paves for the emergence of political-movement. This type of relative-deprivation usually manifests in the form of "Revolutionary Political Movement" as, for instance, there had emerged the French Revolution in 1789, and the Russian Bolshevik Revolution in 1917.

Thus, 'Relative-Deprivation' may take different forms, and accordingly generate political-movement.

9.2.3 Organizational Factor

'Political-Movement' may emerge, in reality, and become manifest only when it is organized. A 'movement' cannot take form, and become dynamic if people's dissatisfaction and frustration against the Political System remains latent and concealed. Therefore, the grievances and demands of the people need to be articulated, and a formal organization[23] needs to be formed for attainment of desired objectives. For this purpose, the political movement is to be organized with precise objectives, enlisted membership, leadership, fund or resources, and strategies of action so that it may strive actively for effective attainment of goals.

9.2.4 Conjunction of Causal Factors

Thus, there may be discerned several causal factors including the structural factor, the socio-psychological factor, and the organizational factor as the vital determinants of emergence and formation of "Political Movement". However, all these factors tend to influence and determine conjointly the genesis of political-movement. Though the socio-psychological factor, and the structural factor seem to constitute the seeds for the genesis of "political-movement", yet it cannot become manifest, dynamic, and effective if it does not have a formal organization. Therefore, the socio-psychological factor, the structural factor, and the organizational factor, in conjunction, seem to contribute towards the genesis and emergence of 'political-movement'.

9.3 Strategies and Techniques

'Political-Movement' may be made dynamic, for attainment of desired objectives or goals, on employing various strategies or plans, methods and techniques of action. In view of their nature, whether pacific or violent, these may be classified broadly into two types such: (i) Non-violent Strategy, and (ii) Violent Strategy.

The chief proponent of the "Non-violent Strategy" is Mohandas Karamchand Gandhi[24] who is popularly known as 'Mahatma Gandhi' and also the Father of the Nation-State of India. This strategy involves the conduct of protests peacefully against the Government or the Authority of the Political System so as to exert moral pressure upon it for bringing about desired reforms and changes. It is essentially characterized by total abnegation and avoidance of violence in thought, words and deeds on the part of the members and leaders of the movement against the incumbents of the Government and its property. Simultaneously, it requires the movement-members and its adherents to have utmost respect and love towards the opponents but to resist actively, with greatest self-control and self-suffering, their unjust policies and evil designs and thereby, to appeal to their heart and to exert moral pressure on them for reforming or changing their misdeeds. Thus, the non-violent strategy is founded upon the fundamental premise of spiritual kinship of all human beings, and emphasizes upon employment of moral means for attaining moral ends. The moral means, or methods and techniques for making the movement dynamic may involve various forms such as '*satyagraha*' (devotion to truth and justice), fasting, non-cooperation and civil-disobedience, and self-imposed sufferings, etc. For this purpose, the movement-adherents work as '*satyagrahis*' devoted completely to the attainment of justice and human-values in the Society and the Polity and they refuse to co-operate with the unjust Government and its functionaries; actively disobey its unjust policies and orders; resort to self-imposed sufferings including fasting; face cheerfully governmental atrocities and cruelties committed on them; and thus, they strive to humanize the opponents, and to convert them to the cause of justice by appealing to their heart.[25] These non-violent techniques and strategies which are spiritual creations of Mohandas Karamchand Gandhi have been practiced by him and the people of India under his towering leadership in organizing and launching in 1921, the "Indian Independence Movement" that culminated successfully in the independence of India from the British-rule on 15th August, 1947.

As distinguished from the 'non-violent strategy', the "violent-strategy" involves employment of methods and techniques of violence and terrorism against the Government for attainment of desired objectives and goals. The chief proponent of this strategy is Karl Marx[26] who emphasizes on armed rebellion as the only effective technique of the proletariat movement for ending class-struggle and exploitation, and for establishing the "Just Communist Society". He believes that just socio-political changes cannot be easily and quickly brought about in the present-day 'Capitalist Society' unless the 'capitalist-class' is completely annihilated and eradicated by the 'proletariat-class', and hence, for attaining the desired objective, the only method is that of revolutionary violence or armed rebellion. The violent strategy as recommended by Marx may be used by the adherents of a political-movement against the Government of the Political System as a pressure-technique for bringing about desired changes in the Society and the Polity. It may take various forms; however, there may be discerned some major types[27] such as: (i) 'Turmoil' that includes strikes, riots, localized rebellion etc. undertaken spontaneously, and in an unorganized manner, (ii) 'Conspiratorial Violence' that includes small scale terrorism, *coup d'etat*, palace-revolts, assassination etc. undertaken in a highly planned and organized manner, and (iii) 'Internal War' that includes large scale terrorism, civil-war, insurgency, and mass-revolution, etc. undertaken in a highly planned, organized and directed manner.

Thus, the 'violet strategy' involves blood-shed, and even loss of life of the opponents, and coerces them physically to bring about socio-political changes as desired by the leaders and adherents of the movement; whereas the 'non-violent strategy' involves active and cheerful self-suffering of the 'movement-adherents' for changing the heart of the opponents and converting them to the movement's cause and objectives in a situation of peace and goodwill. Since change of heart makes for durable change of policies and perspectives, the "non-violent strategy", rather than the "violent strategy", seems to contribute toward durable and effective attainment of the movement's objectives and goals.

9.4 Movement's Effectiveness

The effectiveness or success of a "Political Movement" in attaining its objectives and goals seems to be crucially determined by many and varied factors. However, there may be discerned some major factors such as organizational cohesiveness, physical-resources, political-skill of its leaders, size of its organization, and psychological-resource that tend to be the vital determinants.[28]

For becoming effective, the movement needs to be well-organized and cohesive in the sense that it must have defined, and well-articulated objectives; enlisted membership; a formal structure of authority with centralization of decision-making power in the core-group of leaders; and commitment of its members to the movement's objectives as well as their allegiance to the leaders. However, its organizational-cohesiveness tends to be crucially determined by the extent of intensity of emotional attachment of the members to the movement's objectives and ideology.

The movement, as a challenging group of adherents, also needs physical resources such as wealth or funds, and ownership or control over mass-media. Wealth enables it to meet and defray the expenditures necessary for making it dynamic; and media-ownership or control enables it to publicize its objectives, and to recruit people's support on reaching them easily and quickly, and on indoctrinating them to its cause. Moreover, the size of its organization, whether large or small, in respect of its membership and geographical area of coverage, seems to determine the extent of its effectiveness. A movement which is large in its membership and extensive in geographical area or coverage is likely to exert tremendous pressure upon the Government to pay due attention to its demands; whereas its localized size with smallness of membership may make it less effective. The effectiveness of a movement also tends to be crucially affected by the political-skill of its leaders in devising, designing, and implementing suitable or rational strategies characterized by end-means logic; and also by their capability to motivate and enthuse the adherents to obey their decisions actively and sincerely.

Besides these determinants, however, the most important one seems to be the psychological resource of the movement. It connotes the capital of public goodwill or support that the movement is able to harness and retain with it for furthering its objectives and ideology on pressurizing the Government. Hence, the greater is the capital of public goodwill to its cause, the greater may be the effectiveness of the movement in attaining its goals. Of course, people's support seems to be conditioned mostly by the pattern of societal-culture. For instance, if the 'societal-culture' imbues with the value of 'fatalism' and makes the people believe that every happening in this world is pre-destined and determined by God (as it may be noted in India), people may lack in self-potency and competence, and may become indifferent to worldly-affairs including the problems of life, and the Society as well. Consequently, they may view socio-political ills and evils such as prevalence of injustice, exploitation, corruption, disregard or loss of human values, misrule, and incapacity of the Government etc. with fatalistic resignation; and they may become hesitant to organize a movement for bringing about socio-political changes. Similarly, if the societal-culture imbues with the value of atomistic individualism, the individual tends to be highly 'self-centred', and he may not come forward spontaneously to form a group and organize a movement in co-operation with others.

Thus, the determinants are many and varied. However, conjointly these seem to influence and determine the extent of effectiveness of a 'Political-Movement'.

9.5 Movement and the Political System

Movement is organized for attainment of desired socio-political changes on pressurizing the Political System or transforming it through non-violent methods or violent methods. Since the Government of the Political System is the focal point or target of pressure, the former tends to react to the movement in different yet strategically calculated ways. As it holds sovereign power, and manages the public sphere, it initially tends to resist any collective-action which is undertaken with the intention to reform, challenge, or change its authoritative decisions or structure. Therefore, the initial response of the Political System to the movement seems to be an attitude of indifference. However, as the movement grows with greater intensity and extent, Government may respond to it by way of undertaking measures that vary from dialogue and negotiation to brutal repression of the movement-adherents and activists. Simultaneously, in order to diffuse collective action, the Government may use various tactics of appeasement with doles and concessions to the adherents; and even of co-option of the leaders of the movement in public decision-making bodies. Thus, the measures undertaken by the Government in response to the movement may be many and varied. However, the Government tends to be softer towards a movement which is reform-oriented within the prevailing institutional framework than a movement which is radical in objective, and violent in strategies for attaining the goal of total change or replacement of the prevalent Political System. Of course, the Political System cannot up-root the movement through repressive measures and brutal force as 'will, not force, is the basis of the State'. Hence, the Political system should accord more importance on measures of political-education and socialization than on repressive measures for maintaining itself, or on the contrary, it should change itself in conformity with the demands of its people so as to prevent socio-political upheavals.

REFERENCES

1. Henry Cecil Wyld and Eric H. Patridge (eds), *Webster Universal Dictionary*. (New York: Routledge & Kegan Paul, 1970). p. 911.
2. Rudolf Heberle:
   (i) *Social Movements: An Introduction to Political Sociology*. (NewYork: Appleton-Century-Croft, 1951), p. 6.
   (ii) 'Types and Functions of Social Movements' in David L. Sillls (ed), *International Encylopedia of the Social Sciences*. (NewYork: The Macmillan & the Free Press, 1968), Vol. 14, pp. 438-444.

3. David Easton, *A Systems Analysis of Political Life*. (NewYork: John Wiley & Sons, 1965), p. 165.
4. Andre Gunder Frank & Marte Feuntes: "Nine Theses on Social Movements", *Economic and Political Weekly*, 29th August, 1987, pp. 1503-10.
5. Rudolf Heberle, 'Types and Functions of Social Movements' in David L. Sillls (ed), *International Encylopedia of the Social Sciences*. Vol. 14 (New York: The Macmillan and the Free Press, 1968), p. 439.
6. Paul Wilkinson, *Social Movements*. (London: Pall-Mall, 1971).
7. John Wilson, *Introduction to Social Movements* (New York: Basic Books, 1973).
8. Anthony M. Orum, *Introduction to Political Sociology*. (Englewood Cliffs, N.J.: Prentice-Hall Inc, 1978) p. 342.
9. Rudolf Heberle, 'Types and Functions of Social Movements', *Op. cit.*, pp. 347-366.
10. Anthony M. Orum, *Introduction to Political Sociology. Op. cit.* pp. 347-366.
11. Karl Marx, *The Communist Manifesto*. Reprinted. (Moscow: Progressive Publisher, 1975.
12. Max Weber, *Economy and Society: An Outline of Interpretive Sociology*. Translated by Guenther Ruth and Claus Wittich. (NewYork: Bedminister Press, 1968) Vol. I-III.
13. Ted Robert Gurr, *Why Men Rebel*. (New Jersey: Princeton University Press, 1970). Paperback Edition, 1971, p. 23.
14. Daniel Lerner, *The Passing of Traditional Societies*. (Glencoe, Illinois: The Free Press, 1958).
15. James C. Davies, *When Men Revolt and Why: A Reader in Political Violence and Revolution*. (New York: The Free Press, 1971).
16. W.G. Runciman, *Relative Deprivation and Social Justice*. (London: Routledge & Kegan Paul, 1966).
17. H. Nieburg, *Political Violence: The Behavioural Process*. (New York: St. Martin's Press, 1969).
18. Crane Brinton, *The Anatomy of Revolution*. (NewYork: Random House, 1965).
19. Ted Robert Gurr, *Why Men Rebel*. '*Op. cit.* pp. 47-53.
20. *Ibid.* p. 51.
21. *Ibid.* p. 47.
22. *Ibid.* p. 53.
23. (i) William Gamson, *Power and Discontent*. (Homewood, Illinois: Dorsey Press, 1968).
    (ii) William Gamson, *The Strategy of Social Protest*. (Homewood, Illinois: Dorsey Press, 1975).

(iii) Anthony Oberschall, *Social Conflict and Social Movements*. (Englewood Cliffs, N.J.: Prentice-Hall, 1972).

(iv) Charles Tilly, *The Vendee*. (Cambridge, Mass: Harvard University Press, 1964).

(v) Charles Tilly, Louise Tilly and Richard Tilly, *The Rebellious Century* (Cambridge, Mass: Harvard University Press, 1975).

24. Mohandas Karamchand Gandhi, *An Autobiography or the Story of My Experiments with Truth*. Translated by Mahadev Desai (Ahmedabad: Navajivan Publishing House, 1927).

25. (i) Gopinath Dhawan, *The Political Philosophy of Mahatma Gandhi*. (Ahmedabad: Navajivan Publishing House, 1962). Third Revised Edition.

(ii) D.G. Tendulkar, *Mahatma: Life of Mohandas Karamchand Gandhi* (Delhi: Publications Division, Government of India, 1960) in 8 volumes.

(iii) Krishnalal Shridharani, *War Without Violence—A Study of Gandhi's Method and Its Accomplishments*. (Bombay: Bharatiya Vidya Bhawan, 1962).

(iv) Joan V. Bondurant, *The Conquest of Violence: the Gandhian Philosophy of Conflict*. (Berkeley, CA: University of California Press, 1965).

(v) Gene Sharp, *The Politics of Non-violent Action*. (Boston, MA: Peter Sergent, 1973).

26. Karl Marx, *The Communist Manifesto*. *Op. cit.*

27. (i) Ted Robert Gurr, *Why Men Rebel*. *Op. cit.*

(ii) Anthony M. Orum, *Introduction to Political Sociology*. *Op. cit.* pp. 422-427.

28. (i) Harry Eckstein, *Pressure Group Politics*. (Stanford: Stanford University Press, 1960), pp. 15-39.

(ii) William A. Gamson, *The Strategy of Social Protest*. *Op. cit.*

10

Political Modernization

10.1 The Concept

The nomenclature "Political-Modernization" connotes a societal process through which Politics, at the level of both the individual and the Society, gets modernized. Hence, it may be termed as the process of "Modernization of Politics" that involves acquisition of modern political orientations and behaviour-patterns by the individual, and also acquisition and display of modern structural and functional attributes by the Political System of the Society in response to the challenges of the over-all process of modernization[1]. As "Modernization" constitutes the explanatory variable of Politics in the "Political-Modernization Process", it seems necessary to discern its meaning, scope, and implications.

The term "Modernization" embraces a wide variety of definitions, and there is found no universal consensus on its precise meaning as scholars view it in different perspectives, and formulate different sets of attributes. However, despite proliferation of alternative definitions, it is generally viewed as a process of comprehensive and progressive societal transformation[2] which occurs and proceeds owing to man-kind's quest for new and innovative knowledge acquired through scientific and technological research and investigations. As Cyril E. Black succinctly points out, modernization is "the process by which historically evolved institutions are adapted to the rapidly changing functions that reflect the unprecedented increase in man's knowledge, permitting control over his environment that accompanied the scientific revolution." Its genesis may be traced, according to Black, to the Renaissance that commenced in Western Europe in the Twelfth Century when writings of the ancient Greek and Arabic scholars were translated and made available, and, as a consequence, intellectuals acquired a new sense of re-awakening and search for rational and scientific explanation of physical and social phenomena for betterment of human life. It provided a tremendous stimulus for the growth of natural sciences, and eventually it culminated, in the Sixteenth Century, in the "Scientific Revolution" that formed "a questioning mind" in man, and motivated him to understand all physical and social phenomena on subjecting them to rational scrutiny, and simultaneously, to search for better conditions of human existence as well. All arenas of intellectual activities underwent rapid transformation; and human knowledge on physical and social environment expanded rapidly. The new knowledge was utilized for betterment of material and social conditions of human life. Hence, "the Scientific Revolution" resulted in expansion of literacy and education, growth of mass-media, industrialization, urbanization, increase in trade and commerce, and greater physical, social, and psychic mobility of the people, and their increasing economic development as well. These new happenings challenged the traditional way of life of the people and the traditional institutions of the Society, and necessitated their adaptation with the changing societal environment. Thus, there commenced the process of comprehensive and progressive societal transformation which is termed as "Modernization".

These observations of Cyril E. Black are also echoed and upheld by a number of scholars of international eminence. For instance, Daniel Lerner[4] envisions "Modernization" as a multi-dimensional process of societal change involving changes in all institutions of Society as well as the attitudes and behaviour of its people. According to him, the prime-mover of "modernization" is the need for economic growth and development which is sought to be attained through technological advancement and industrialization. For this purpose, there need be brought about relevant changes in the values, skills, and dispositions of the people. These changes tend to challenge and influence all traditional institutions of the Society, and to pave for the emergence of "Modern Society" characterized by self-sustaining growth in economy, public participation in the polity, diffusion of secular-rational norms in the culture, increment of mobility of the individual in the sense of personal freedom of physical, social, and psychic movement, and formation of modal personality that equip him to function effectively in a social order that operates according to the foregoing characteristics[5]. Similarly, Wilbert E. Moore[6], and S.N. Eisenstadt[7] also view "modernization" as a multi-faceted and complex process of societal transformation that enhances human well-being both materially and culturally. It involves structural changes in all institutions and systems of the Society as well as changes in all areas of human thought and behaviour for enhancing the quality of human life and existence. As a consequence, there emerges "The Modern Society" having the ability not only to develop institutional structure for adjusting to, and absorbing these continuous changes but also to maintain civil order and social stability without any disorganization, chaos, and disintegration.

Thus, an analysis of these notions and views reveal that modernization is a multi-dimensional process involving changes, for betterment, in all aspects of human thought and activities as well as in all areas of Society. Therefore, there may be discerned some salient attributes of modernity which may be acquired and developed through the process of modernization. At the level of the individual, modernization infuses in his mind a scientific temper characterized by an attitude for rational enquiry. As a consequence, he forms an "analytico-causal out-look"[8]; develops a conviction that nothing happens without a cause; and he seeks to understand and explain every phenomenon,—whether physical, biological, or social, on subjecting it to rational enquiry, scrutiny, and analysis. He is, thus, motivated to find out the inherent correlationship between "cause" and "effect" on the concerned phenomenon, and searches out measures for bettering the conditions of human life. Accordingly, he devises and employs scientific methods of enquiry embodying rational and universal norms in order to understand and explain all phenomena, and incessantly works, with a sense of competence and efficacy, for controlling or changing these to suit to his needs and necessities. Thus, modernization brings about a fundamental shift in the values, attitudes, and out-look of the individual. Therefore, a modern individual believes in the possibility and desirability of changing natural and societal environment, and he becomes change-prone, active, and participant in his approach to life and problems around him[9]; whereas a traditional individual remains passive, acquiescent, change-resistant and *status-quoist*, both psychologically and behaviourally; and lacking in self-competence, he expects and accepts continuity in nature and societal life. These changes in the psychology of a modern individual tend to influence his intellectual endeavours, and there occurs tremendous expansion of knowledge on natural and societal environment, and its diffusion in Society through increased literacy, education, and mass-communications.[10] Simultaneously, it facilitates formation of a "Culture" that imbues with the values of rationalism, secularism, humanism, and nouminal individuality[11].

Modernization of the individual, of course, affects all systems and institutions of the Society owing to the fact that these become operative and dynamic when individuals, as their members, play relevant roles. In this context, at the level of the Social System, modernization brings about increased occupational, social, and geographic mobility; a marked increase in people's health and life-expectancy; increasing urbanization involving a rapid growth of urban population, and cities and townships; formation of functionally specific secondary groups and associations in increasing number and variety that supplement the traditional and primary groups such as family and kinship groups having diffuse roles; and a re-organization of the social system on the basis of the principles of structural-differentiation, and functional-specificity[12]. At the level of the Economic System, modernization brings about rapid growth in industrialization; decline in the significance of agriculture compared to industrial, commercial, and non-agricultural activities; centralization of economic activities at the national level with the emergence of national market, national sources of capital, and other national economic institutions; diversification of occupational activities with new skills and expertise; increasing per capita income and gross national product; and emergence of an economic system characterized by self-sustaining growth and continual increase in both production and consumption[13].

Thus, modernization brings about new and significant changes not only in the psychology and intellect of the individual but also in the structure and functions of the Social System as well as the

Economic System of the Society. Consequently, there also commences, as Karl W. Deutsch terms it, a process of "Social mobilization" that tends to challenge the Political System and entails serious implications for it. Hence, in order to resolve these challenges, the Political System is required to modernize itself suitably; and there ensues the process of "Political Modernization".

10.2 Political Modernization

Political-modernization is a distinct dimension of the process of societal modernization. It is that process through which the Political System of the Society gets modernized, and its political actors acquire attributes of modernity. In this context, the stimuli for bringing about relevant changes in the structure and functions of the Political System seem to emanate from the process of societal modernization as it entails stupendous challenges that tend to affect adversely political stability, viability, and development.

10.2.1 Modernization's Implications on Politics

The process of modernization brings about "Social Mobilization"[14] through which, as Karl W. Deutsch point out, "major clusters of old social, economic, and psychological commitments are either eroded or broken and people become available for new patterns of socialization and behaviour."[15] Thus, there occurs significant and drastic changes in the attitude, values, and expectation of the people from those associated with the traditional life to those of a modern life due to expansion of literacy and education, increased communications, media-exposure, and urbanization. Therefore, the traditional individual, on being exposed to new styles of life, new standard of material enjoyment and new possibilities for their satisfaction, obtain new experiences that break decisively the cognitive and attitudinal barriers of the traditional culture, and that generate in him new aspirations and wants in order to live a modern life. On the whole, the people of a traditional society become socially mobilized with new aspirations and expectations, and make huge demands on the Political System for providing positive opportunities and amenities for their realization. However, the traditional or the transitional Political System finds itself unable to fulfil their increasing aspirations and demands owing to its lower level of economic development. Hence, when 'social mobilization' far exceeds 'economic development' of the Society, there emerges a wide-gap between people's aspirations and the Government's performance; between want-formation and want-satisfaction; and this gap generates social frustration and dissatisfaction. Moreover, people become increasingly frustrated when they find themselves deprived of occupational and social mobility opportunities for fulfilling their aspirations. In such a situation, when 'social frustration' far exceeds 'mobility-opportunities', people tend to make a huge number of demands on the Government of the Political System; and their participation in the political process becomes unruly and aggressive. Such unconventional and violent political participation of the people tends to challenge the "Constitutional Order" that contains the fundamental rules of the political game for making and implementing authoritative public policies for the Society. Consequently, the Political System experiences tremendous stresses and difficulties in undertaking "authoritative allocation of values" for the Society as its "political-institutionalization" (legitimacy) is seriously undermined; and there emerges a situation of political instability and disorder. Hence, when 'political-participation' far exceeds 'political-institutionalization', the outcome would be, most likely, 'political instability' born out of failure of the Political System to maintain socio-political order, and this situation may eventually pave for disintegration of the Society. The adverse impact of modernization on politics is succinctly pointed out by Samuel P. Huntington[16] in the following formulation:

1. $$\frac{\text{Social mobilization}}{\text{Economic development}} = \text{Social frustration}$$

2. $$\frac{\text{Social frustration}}{\text{Mobility opportunities}} = \text{Political participation}$$

2. $$\frac{\text{Political Participation}}{\text{Political Institutionalization}} = \text{Political participation}$$

Thus, the process of modernization that brings about social mobilization may produce disastrous consequences for the Political System, and may challenge its stability and viability. Since the root cause of political instability is economic under-development of the Society, and incapacity of the Political System to satisfy the ever-increasing aspirations and demands of the people, the Political System is required to restructure and modernize itself for bringing about people's economic development[17].

10.2.2 Emergence of Modern Political System

The impetus for the emergence of a "Modern Political System", thus, seems to emanate from the pressing need for economic development for fulfilling the increasing aspirations and demands of the people as caused by the process of societal modernization. Of course, economic development of the Society involves both industrial development and agricultural development which, in turn, demand free-flow of ideas on modern techniques and methods, born out of continuous scientific innovations and research, for use in the productive process. It also, simultaneously, demands decentralization of decision-making power, on the basis of expertise and skills, in the productive process. These requirements of economic development, in both the industrial and the agricultural sectors, however, may be fulfilled in a Society provided its Political System is restructured and modernized as a liberal democratic system, what David E. Apter terms as the "Reconciliation model" of Political System[18] characterized principally by "pyramidal authority-structure" and "instrumental value-system". It recognizes and upholds the value of the individual's autonomy and dignity on considering him as an end, and also on considering the Political System as merely a means or an instrument for attainment of this end. Accordingly, it prescribes for a "Governmental Authority-Structure" which is 'pyramidal' in form in the sense that the Government is based on the consent of the sovereign people, and that the legitimate power of governance flows from the people gradually upward to the top of the Government. Therefore, the 'pyramidal authority-structure' of the Government provides for fundamental rights and liberties to the people, decentralization of political decision-making power, and free-flow of information from the external environment to the Society and within the Society itself.

This "Reconciliation model" of the Political System, as Apter rightly believes, is most suited to bring about economic development of the Society because it tends to democratize the productive process on allowing free-flow of information, and also decentralization of decision-making power in it on the basis of relevant expertise and skills. Democratization of the Political System, thus, seems to influence and facilitate the process of political modernization. In this context Lucian W. Pye also asserts: "...there is a close relationship between democratization and modernization."[19] As such, when the Political System is democratically restructured in conformity with the "Reconciliation model", it may be adorned with the attributes of modernity, and in this process of political modernization, it may attain a developed status. Hence, with the emergence of a "Modern Political System", there may occur its "Political Development".[20]

10.3 Political Development and Political Modernization

The term "Political Development" is usually understood and comprehended as development of the Political System of a National Society. Of course, on the attributes of political development, there is noticed no universal consensus, rather semantic disagreement among scholars. However, a large number of scholars seems to accept and recognize the "Development-Syndrome" conceptualized by the Comparative Politics Committee of the Social Science Research Council of U.S.A. as the most relevant and useful theoretical construct for measuring the level of development of a National Political System. The "Development Syndrome" provides for a measuring scale that consists of three major indicators or determinants such as: (1) Equality, (2) Capacity or Capability, and (3) Differentiation with Specialization[21] which may be conjointly employed for measuring the level of development of the Political System of a National Society. The level of " Equality" may be measured in respect of three dimensions such as: (i) the nature and extent of political participation, (ii) the nature of the legal system, and (iii) the nature of the public recruitment system. In this context, 'Political Development', as per the determinant of Equality, firstly requires that the Political System must uphold and practice the principles of political equality and liberty of its citizens so as to enable them to participate freely and equally in its political process. It requires spontaneous, active, and extensive participation of the people in political arenas; for instance, they are required to participate actively, equally, and freely in the electoral process in voting and electing their representatives to form the government; in ventilating their demands and grievances to the government for redress; and in forming political parties and groups etc. As regard this dimension, the attributes of development are free, equal, active, and extensive participation of the people in the political process. Secondly, as regard the legal system, development is characterized by the attributes of rationality, universality, and secularity. The laws enacted by the Political System must be founded on right reason and interests of all its citizens; be universal in application on upholding the principles of rule of law, and equality before law; and be secular, not theocratic, in content. Thirdly, as regard the public recruitment system, development requires it to be achievement-oriented in the sense that recruitment to public offices, both civil and military, must be made on the basis of achievement and merit of the candidates adjudged through open competitive examinations, not on ascriptive considerations of class, status, or heritage.

The second major determinant of "Political Development" is the Political System's capacity or capability which connotes its over-all performance as a distinct unit in the environment for attainment of societal goals. It may be empirically measured in respect of four dimensions such as: (i) extractive capability, (ii) regulative capability, (iii) distributive capability, and (iv) responsive capability. In this context, firstly, the Political System is required to possess high extractive capability in the sense of extracting, from its people, necessary goods and services in the form of taxes and personnel for discharging all its civil and military functions. Secondly, the Political System is required to possess high regulative capability in the sense of regulating effectively any unruly and deviant behaviour of its citizens as necessary for maintaining law and order, peace, and stability in the Society. Thirdly, the Political System is required to possess high distributive capability in the sense of providing equitable distribution of public goods and resources among the people through enactment and effective implementation of public welfare schemes and measures. Fourthly, the Political System is required to possess high responsive capability in the sense of actively responding to people's opinion, and remaining responsible to them for all its acts of omissions and commissions. Thus, "Political Development" requires that all these four types of capabilities must be displayed, to a great extent, in the over-all performance of the Political System. However, among these, the most crucial one is the responsive capability as it tends to generate and foster in the people a high sense of patriotism that spontaneously motivates them to legitimize the Political System. Consequently, on being legitimized, the Political System is enabled to acquire and retain (i) high level of extractive capability as people tend to pay taxes and render services to it willingly and regularly; (ii) high level of regulative capability as they abide by its laws, rules, and regulations spontaneously, and help it to maintain peace, order, and harmony in the Society; (iii) and high level of distributive capability for distributing the extracted resources equitably among the people through enactment and effective implementation of public welfare schemes. Therefore, high level of responsive capability seems to be the most important and crucial variable of development of a Political System.

The third major determinant of 'Political Development" is the level of "Differentiation with Specialization" that characterizes the "Structural-Functional Relationship" in the Political System. It connotes the level of "structural-differentiation, and functional-specificity and specialization" in the context of the dynamics of Political System in processing 'inputs' and producing 'outputs'. For becoming dynamic, the Political System is required to perform seven major types of functions such as political socialization and recruitment, political communication, interest-articulation, interest-aggregation, rule-making, rule-application, and rule-adjudication. These functions are universal to all Political Systems, yet development requires that each of these functions must be performed by a distinct and specialized structure. For this purpose, there must be formed relevant political-infrastructures such as political-socialisers and recruitment agencies, mass-media, pressure groups, political parties, legislature, executive, and judiciary, with necessary specialization and autonomy, for performing respectively the functions of political-socialization and recruitment, political-communication, interest-articulation, interest-aggregation, rule-making, rule-application, and rule-adjudication. Each of these structures must have a distinct identity and autonomy in the sense of being different from other structures, and specialize in its specific function without interfering in the functions of other structures. As such, "Political Development" requires that a high level of "structural-differentiation with functional-specificity and specialization" must characterize the pattern of "Structural-Functional Relationship" in a Political System.

Thus, the level of "Political Development" may be empirically measured conjointly on the basis of the attributes of development that pertain to the dimensions of equality, systemic-capability, and structural-differentiation with functional-specialization in a Political-System. Of course, these development attributes tend to characterize its edifice or institutional arrangement and behavioural pattern that, however, would become evident, in reality, provided the socio-political culture of the people takes the form of Democratic Political Culture or "Civic Culture"[22]. The "Civic Culture" is essentially an "allegiant-participant[23]" political culture, and is characterized by rationalistic and nationalistic orientations as well as liberal-democratic values. Hence, it tends to motivate the people not only to will for the "Reconciliation Model" of the Political System characterized by "instrumental value-system" and "pyramidal authority-structure" but also to play relevant political roles in order to maintain and develop it. Hence, "the Civic Culture" that imbues with modern attributes seems to be the most important determinant of "Political Development" as well as "Political Modernization". It tends not only to make the individual political actor modern in orientations and dispositions but also to motivate the mass of political actors or people to form for them a Political System adorned with modern structural and functional attributes. Therefore, only when the "Civic Culture" is formed in the people, there may emerge a "Modern Political System" with capacity to solve the challenges of societal modernization, and simultaneously, there may ensue the process of its "Political Development".

Therefore, the study and analysis of the "Political-Modernization Phenomenon" necessarily involves empirical investigations into the process of 'Modernization of Politics' including implications of 'Societal modernization on Politics', and also the emergence of a 'Modern Political System' adorned with the attributes of 'Political Development'.

REFERENCES

1. (i) Samuel P. Huntington, *Political Order in Changing Societies.* (New Haven: Yale University Press, 1968) p. 34.
   (ii) David E. Apter, *The Politics of Modernization.* (Chicago: Chicago University Press, 1965) p. 24/25.
2. Cyril E. Black, *The Dynamics of Modernization.* (New York: Harper & Row, 1967) p. 7. First published in 1966.
3. *Ibid.* p. 7.
4. (i) Daniel Lerner, *The Passing of Traditional Society.* (Glencoe, Illinois: Free Press, 1958) p. 438.
   (ii) 'Modernization: Social Aspects', in David L. Sills (ed), *International Encyclopaedia of Social Sciences* (New York: Macmillan & Free Press, 1968) pp. 386-395, especially, p. 392.
5. Daniel Lerner, 'Modernization: Social Aspects.' *op. cit.*; p. 387.
6. Wilbert E. Moore, *Social Change.* (Englewood Cliffs, N.J.: Prentice-Hall, 1963).
7. S.N. Eisenstadt, *Modernization-Protest and Change.* (Englewood Cliffs, N.J.: Prentice-Hall, 1966), pp. 2-4, and 41-42.
8. (i) James O' Connell, 'The Concept of Modernization', in Cyril E. Black (ed), *Comparative Modernization.* (New York: Free Press, 1976) p. 6.
   (ii) Alex Inkeles, 'A Model of the Modern Man', in Nancy Hammond (ed), *Social Science and the New Societies.* (East Lancing: Social Science Research Bureau, Michigan State University, 1973), pp. 59-92.
9. Alex Inkeles, 'A Model of the Modern Man.' *op. cit.*; pp. 59-92.
10. Daniel Lerner, The Passing of Traditional Society. *op. cit.*.
11. Daniel Lerner, *Ibid.*
12. Marion Levy, *Modernization and the Structure of Societies.* Princeton: Princeton University Press, 1966).
13. (i) R.F. Harrod, *Towards a Dynamic Economics* (London: Macmillan, 1951).
    (ii) Albert O Hirschman, Strategy of Economic Development.(New Haven: Yale University Press, 1958).
    (iii) W.W. Rostow: *The Stages of Economic Growth.* (Cambridge: Cambridge University Press, 1960).
    (iv) Robert T. Holt and John E. Turner, *The Political Basis of Economic Development.* (Princeton: D. Von Nostrand, 1966).
14. Karl W. Deutsch, 'Social Mobilization and Political Development'. *American Political Science Review*, 55, September 1961.
15. *Ibid.* p. 494.

16. Samuel P. Huntington, *Political Order in Changing Societies. op. cit.*; p. 55.
17. David E. Apter, *The Politics of Modernization. op. cit.*
18. *Ibid.* pp. 22, 25, 398-399.
19. Lucian W. Pye, *Aspects of Political Development.* (Boston: Little, Brown & Co, 1966) Indian Edn. published by Amerind Publishing Co.; New Delhi, 1972, p. 81.
20. (i) *Ibid.* p. 45.
    (ii) Lucian W. Pye, Leonard Binder, James S. Coleman, Joseph La Palombara, Sidney Verba and Myron Weiner (eds), *Crises and Sequences in Political-Development.* (Princeton, N.J.: Princeton University Press, 1971).
21. Lucian W. Pye, *Aspects of Political Development.* Indian Edn; *Op. cit.* pp. 45-47.
22. (i) *Ibid.* pp. 47-48.
    (ii) Gabriel A. Almond and Sidney Verba: *The Civic Culture.* (Princeton, N.J.: Princeton University Press, 4th Printing, 1972) pp. 21, 31, 476, 498. First published in 1963.
23. Gabriel A. Almond and Sidney Verba, *The Civic Culture. Op. cit.* pp. 31-32.

Index